Ministry Among Students

Simon Robinson is Chaplain of Leeds University

Ministry Among Students

*A Pastoral Theology
and Handbook
for Practice*

Simon Robinson

CANTERBURY
PRESS
Norwich

First published in 2004 by the Canterbury Press Norwich
(a publishing imprint of Hymns Ancient & Modern Limited,
a registered charity)
St Mary's Works, St Mary's Plain,
Norwich, Norfolk, NR3 3BH

www.scm-canterburypress.co.uk

British Library Cataloguing in Publication data

A catalogue record for this book is available
from the British Library

ISBN 1-85311-582-7

Typeset by Regent Typesetting, London
Printed and bound by
Biddles Ltd, www. biddles.co.uk

Contents

Dedication

This book is dedicated to the two students who have taught me the most, my daughter Sarah, who got her degree about a year ago, and my son Jamie, who at the time of writing is facing the toils of 'freshers' week'. The joy they have given me knows no bounds, not because of what they have achieved, but because of who they are, and how they constantly surprise me.

Introduction

Now is the time to focus on student ministry. With some four million students in Further Education and with a government target of half 18–30 year olds to be in Higher Education by 2010, there has never been a better time to set in place effective mission. In parish work and university chaplaincy there is the chance to get alongside very many people who are in transition and, as such, reflecting on what is important to them. Traditionally work with students has tended to be quite narrow, with a strong emphasis either on youth work approaches or upon nurturing future church leaders from the intelligentsia. The challenge of present day Higher and Further Education is now to use the imagination to reach out beyond the narrow confines of the Church and engage with more students directly. The message of this book is that to do this effectively the Church has to take seriously and relate creatively to the students' whole environment, including the academic, administrative, support and managerial staff. It also requires that parish and chaplaincy work together as an effective team, developing and building on different networks. The wider the networks, the better the outreach.

I hope this book then will be useful to three groups: Higher and Further Education chaplains and chaplaincy assistants, anyone who works with students in a voluntary or church capacity, and those who appoint chaplains and determine how they fit in with local mission.

For HE and FE chaplains I hope the book will provide stimulation to develop ministry and make connections. It is not a simple blueprint for chaplaincy work. There can be no such thing. There are a number of different kinds of universities, and the dynamic now is to squeeze HE and FE into four leagues:

- Universities majoring in research.
- Universities with a good mixture of research and teaching.

- Universities which are all teaching, and which major in vocational courses.
- Further Education colleges, which deliver a great number of HE modules, feed many students into HE, and focus on vocational courses.

The first two tend to have space for extracurricular events. The third, approximating to the old polytechnics, have little space for extracurricular activities and do not have a culture of involved students. This is taken further by the Further Education colleges. They have little time for extracurricular activities but because of their flexibility are very much central to the local community.

What is surveyed in this book gives a number of different strategies that can be applied to any or all of the different institutions. Where there is little space outside the curriculum, for instance, the chaplaincy can become involved in the curriculum in such a way that it is asking the same questions about spiritual meaning and how this applies to vocation and to industry. I do not deal at any length specifically with FE as such, but all strategies are transferable.

In all this the watchword of chaplaincy is 'connect'. How can the chaplaincy team connect to different activities and enable spiritual reflection in any situation, be that in the curriculum, the coffee bar or the chapel?

This book is also for anyone who works in the local church or voluntary sector with students. While the primary perspective is from HE chaplaincy, it attempts to show how this fits into church work and how local churches can play an important part in caring for the students in their town. Hence, from the perspective of local church workers it provides pathways to linking into student support and care and into the professional support structure. The chapters on, for example, student culture and pastoral and worship needs are relevant to any student workers.

Finally, this book is for all who make church policies in this area. Their decisions will determine how the Church as a whole responds to what is the quickest growing sector of education in the UK. Hence, there is the need to know something of the possibilities that are there for including them in mission strategies. They may not work directly with students but they do facilitate that work and enable it to be connected to the overall mission of the Church.

The focus is on practice, with theology emerging from and informing that practice.

The book is divided into four parts:

- The context of student ministry.
- Priestly work.
- Pastoral work.
- Prophetic work.

Part 1 begins to look at student culture in all its complexity. Chapter 2 looks at how the chaplaincy can begin to establish recognition in the institution. It aims to show how the work of chaplains has to be anchored in both the church and the educational institution, and how this can be developed. It also looks at the basic framework of teamwork, arguing that an ecumenical team is critical to inclusive mission.

Chapter 3 aims to establish the foundation of an underlying practical theology that looks at how chaplaincy can enable the public communication of God among students and in the institution.

Part 2 of the book, on the priestly work of chaplaincy, consists of two chapters, on worship and building bridges. Chapter 4 argues that worship is central to the public communication of God on campus, and outlines different ways in which it might be established and developed. Chapter 5 then argues that the bridges created by networking are not just a nice addition to the work of chaplaincy but rather its lifeblood, enabling dialogue and communication as well as effective collaboration with the different communities that go to make up the life of a university and thus to make up the life of the student.

Part 3 involves three chapters focusing on pastoral work, first with traditional students, then with staff and postgraduates, and finally with international students. In each of these chapters my aim is to show something of the problems faced by these very different groups of students, to offer some examples of how chaplaincy can respond from its own resources and in collaboration with others, on and off campus, and to say something about the distinctive nature of spiritual and pastoral care as offered by the chaplaincy.

Part 4 looks at the prophetic activity of chaplaincy. I consider this in different aspects, how this might be a function of several different groups, and how this might fit into the rest of the Church's mission on campus. Chapter 10 is on curriculum involvement. This is quite a recent innovation, at least done in any systematic way, and I examine how it can enable public dialogue on spirituality and prophetic reflection, and how it links into the different aspects of ministry.

Chapter 11 is an overview of ministry to students and invites the Church as a whole to see how work with students is central to the future of its mission and is essentially collaborative, within and outside the Church.

Finally, an appendix looks at the history of Higher Education institutions, and how the Church has responded.

All the cases I use are factual, with no reference to real names or context. The examples of practice are from different chaplaincies, with a majority from the experience of different teams in Leeds. Leeds has a single team that serves both a traditional university and a more recent one. I have learned more than I could say from all the chaplains in that team over the past twelve years, and wish to thank them all.

Part 1

The Context of
Student Ministry

Student Culture

A former Lord Mayor of Leeds recounts how as a member of an intermediate care team he was with a colleague looking out for available 'half way' houses for ex-psychiatric patients. They discovered one house that looked perfect. As they went in to check it out the curtains twitched in the house next door and they knew that they would have to explain their purpose. They could just hear all the suspicion and fear that usually accompanies the news that ex-psychiatric patients are going to be living next door. By the time they came out of the house there was a little old white haired lady on the doorstep, who met them with a concerned look. With heavy hearts they told her all. Instantly, a beatific smile crossed her lips and she said, 'That's wonderful, I was worried it might have been students.'

It is very tempting to buy into the stereotypical view of students and the student lifestyle. Yes, we all know that students are loud, lazy, drink too much, inhale a variety of toxic substances, lead a hedonistic, irresponsible lifestyle, never thinking of anyone else but themselves, and have no sexual morals.

This view often sits alongside the traditional picture of a three-year residential degree course being part of the leaving home process for mostly middle-class children. The university provides a safe environment to live independently, and to experiment with ideas and behaviour.

The truth is, of course, that student culture is different and far more complex than this picture, and this chapter will give a brief indication of that complexity. It will first outline the postmodern experience which provides the background to Higher Education. Then it will look at how this is embodied in the Student Union. Finally, it will examine:

- The educational culture.
- Lifestyle and living, including finance and debt.
- Life meaning and spirituality, including the religious culture of students.

The Postmodern Context

Scholars argue fiercely about whether we are in so-called postmodern times and if so how such a world might be characterized (Connor 1989). It is, however, possible to distinguish between postmodernity as a theory and the experience of the postmodern era. In the first of these, new ways of understanding language and social constructs are argued for. Baudrillard, for instance, sees the division between art and life as breaking down (Baudrillard 1983). There is no objective sense of reality and each person has to create their own reality and underlying life meaning. Whether or not we agree with such theory it is hard not to accept something of the postmodern *experience*, in which old certainties have broken down. Such an age is characterized by:

- An explosion of scientific and technological progress, making resources available that were undreamed of even fifty years ago. At the same time this leads to a stress on rights and choice, such as the Patient's Charter.
- An increasing influence of theories which stress relativity, indeterminacy or chaos. These began with Freud and his stress on the unconscious, culminating in the postmodern thinkers such as Derrida (Reader 1997).
- A breakdown of patterns of behaviour and institutions such as marriage and the family, caused partly by increased wealth and mobility, but also by changes in attitude towards the sanctity of marriage and the notion of securing a partnership for life.
- A greater development and awareness of cultural and religious diversity within society, caused by increased migration and global awareness.

All of this has led to a breakdown of any sense of objective knowledge and in particular adherence to the so-called 'grand narratives' of the last century. Grand narratives are those 'stories' which claim some universal truth (Lyotard 1979). They range from views about the person – characterized after the Enlightenment as autonomous rational decision maker – to views about the purpose of humanity – dominated in the West by the Christian ethic.

Such grand narratives might exist in the minds of the great thinkers or they might give meaning and purpose to whole nations that help to sustain them through times of crisis. The grand narrative of the British Empire, for instance, gave meaning to the people of Britain and beyond, undergirding the initial acceptance of the sacrifice of so many in the First World War. In turn beneath this was a Christian ethic that had been dominant in the West.

We no longer buy into those narratives. So much of the cultural and economic underpinning has gone. Major conflagrations such as the First World War raised questions about the underlying assumptions, leading eventually to a greater stress on individualism and the values of the free market. The grand narratives have been replaced by many different narratives, both local and national. There are still major narratives, including national loyalty, consumerism, the free market and the more communitarian views (with a stress on the importance on the development of community). However, these are either in competition or dialogue (Brueggemann 1997, 718ff.). None of these narratives are more acceptable than the other and there are no privileged interpreters of any meaning.

Student Union

Walk into any half-functioning student union and you will see the epitome of the postmodern. The many different student groups reflect a radical pluralism. Cheek by jowl with the ballroom dancing society may be the pagan society, with a softness for Aleister Crowley. Even such groups tend not to be univocal, with a mixture of paganism, wicca, as well as more occult interests.

In this experience several things stand out:

- A strong liberal view which sees moral preferences almost as a matter of personal taste. Any perspective of life is as good as another. Tolerance and liberalism are at the heart of any shared view of values, stressing diversity.
- A strong emphasis on the protection of student rights. Where the

rights of students, especially minority groups, are infringed the
union will support them or discipline any union group who might
be responsible.
- A strong sense of customer care. Many unions do their own
  market research to ensure that customer needs are established and
  fulfilled.
- Representation of students. The union is keen to guard student
  autonomy, and will provide representation in academic and
  finance appeals, and in relation to accommodation.
- Welfare and student support. The union has the best advisory
  service on most campuses, ranging from debt management to
  housing advice. There is also often the provision of student
  personal development programmes.
- A concern for educational campaigns in areas such as mental or
  sexual health.

All kinds of different narratives are encouraged within the union
and the union itself has several different narratives it has to hold
together, from student support to maintaining a profit, to customer
care. Inevitably in that context all kinds of value conflicts can
emerge such as the occasion when several student unions decided to
provide funds for students who wanted an abortion. The autonomy
of the student then began to conflict with values such as equality,
and particular values about the sanctity of life from different groups
within the union.

While the student union is in one sense buzzing with different
groups and is open to dialogue, it must also be said that alongside
this is evidence on many campuses of student apathy. There is little
evidence of the political passion of the sixties and seventies which
fuelled student sit-ins, and issue-led extraordinary general meetings
can often be not quorate.

The Context of Education

If the student gets her first view of university life in the Union she is
soon pitched into the experience of learning itself. With the tremen-
dous increase in student numbers we are now into a world of mass
education. This involves much bigger institutions, and with that a
sense of impersonal distance. The sheer size of many universities now

is daunting. One English university is the equivalent of a sizeable town with as many phone points as Selby.

For all students there is distance built into the experience of the curriculum, with less and less staff contact time. The experience of the tutorial is dwindling in most universities, yet many students come with the expectation that there will be close contact with teachers. Personal tutors are under much more stress to produce research and thus are often not available for students in a pastoral role. This means that the student is less likely to use the academic staff as a pastoral resource. In turn this has meant a greater reliance upon the student support services. Even the development of learning skills is increasingly seen as situated outside the academic department, with learning skills centres being established. All this further tends to compartmentalize the academic and the personal, or pastoral. What was integrated in practice is now fragmented. Departments are constantly trying to fulfil pastoral responsibilities, but the strains to produce research and to retain students are immense.

A major reason for student drop-out – mostly in the first term – is precisely because they find it hard to make sense of the size of the university and above all can find no sense of community or friendship, either in the department or outside it (Thomas 2002).

The development of two semesters from three terms and in particular the development of the module system has had major effect on the student experience in two ways. First, the student cannot get away with not attending lectures and seminars. All departments now take seriously the attendance of students, not least to make sure that the student is keeping up work. This puts regular pressure on the student to perform. Second, it is now much more difficult to catch up at the end of the academic year. Judgment comes at the end of each semester. The size of the courses also puts greater strain on resources, making it often hard for the student to get hold of books. However, modularization also brings greater choice and flexibility.

Alongside these pressures there has been a growth in a more utilitarian and consumerist ethos. A good degree is a must for decent employment. Hence, a lot of students feel the need to work harder more regularly. Moreover, given the charging of fees and the loss of the old grants there is a strong sense that the student is not so much in a community of learning as in a contract, in which the staff part is to ensure a good pass.

Hence, parents have become much more vociferous and concerned about their children being given value for money. Whereas open days two decades ago were largely populated by students, there is now a majority of parents. The two questions they most ask are about finance and accommodation. It is likely that this consumerist ethos will become even more pronounced with probability of tuition fees increasing.

With all this there is much more stress on the views of the consumers, with focus groups and other market research organized by the student union, student evaluation forms for all modules, and even in some universities well-being surveys. This consumer ethos is further enhanced by the recent stress on student retention by the Higher Education Funding Council for England (HEFCE). The loss of any student involves significant financial loss, hence departments aim to do all they can to satisfy customers. Hence, many universities include in their planning documents concern for the 'best student experience'.

Barnett (2000) notes that the student is faced with curricula that are trying to make sense of a supercomplex world. A complex world is one in which we are assailed by massive amounts of data, which can be handled through conventional frameworks. A supercomplex world is one in which the amount of data is such that even the frameworks cannot handle it. This leads to attempts to develop high skills and a value-added economy which stress both the importance of distinguishing the very different areas of knowledge and the skills required to develop these (the knowledge society), and the importance of the development of more generic skills, which can enable flexibility, adaptability and self-reliance (Barnett 2000). This leads to greater demands for the curriculum to develop such generic skills. There is much debate as to what these skills are and whether they are narrowly focused around work, or whether they have a more holistic foundation.

Whatever the conclusion, the student is increasingly being asked to reflect in a holistic way on both the content of his course and also on the development of such generic skills. This leads to the developing of reflective learning skills, of learning how to learn, and thus links easily into personal development in a way not systematically done before. This work is being focused on in 'personal-development planning', in which the student sets out a learning agreement and develops a portfolio which integrates his extracurricular life with the curriculum work and focuses on the development of autonomy in relation to work (Baldwin 2003, L5).

There is a view that the very culture of universities is changing because of the widening of participation. This whole issue is under review. In one respect it is very visible. Some 3 per cent of students have some form of disability. In some universities the proportion is as high as 6 per cent. There is also a significant increase in international students, who with their strong work ethic contribute towards the culture of learning.

However, in terms of class it is not so clear that the student experience is being affected by widening participation. First, the 2003 Student Living Report (UNITE 2003) notes that despite the attempt to widen participation there has been little success in terms of encouraging those from the C2, D and E socio-economic backgrounds. The report (with surveys conducted by Mori) shows that 83 per cent of students come from A, B and C1 backgrounds. The 17 per cent from C2, D and E backgrounds are one percentage point down from the previous wave of students. In some more modern universities widening participation is more pronounced.

Lifestyle and Finance

Finance and Debt

Finance is one of the key elements of the student experience and lifestyle. The picture painted a decade ago was of so-called student poverty. The UNITE Report (2003) indicates that the average amount of student debt is almost £5,000, while students anticipate owing over £9,000 once they leave university. The debt issue is the one that is of most concern for the student. This leads to the need to take employment while at university. Over two-fifths of students in the UNITE Report noted that this affected their study adversely. Further analysis reveals once again that students from working-class backgrounds are more likely to be in employment. It is they, on the whole, who report the need to work to supplement their student loan and even to pay tuition fees. A and B background students (44 per cent overall) see employment as a means of keeping up a lifestyle that they have become accustomed to. A quarter see employment as good experience and as looking good on the CV. This is also reflected in the view of 80 per cent that they are managing their finances well. This reflects a feeling that for all the problems about debt and finance the majority see it simply as part of their money management. A culture of debt has suddenly arisen which the majority of students simply accept as given. For many students this has led to weekends dominated by employment. Some students even go home at weekends because this is where they can find the best employment. Once more such patterns work against the development of the old forms of a learning community.

Those who suffer most from finance-related stress are the working-class students and those who have little capacity to manage their finances. It is mostly working-class students who have thought about leaving university, due to money problems. The debate continues about the effect of debt on the less well off. It is calculated that the average graduate will earn more than £400,000 over a life time. The problem is that many non-traditional graduates are not getting the jobs they had hoped for.

'Cigareetes and whuskey and wild, wild women'

We cannot avoid the hedonistic element in the lifestyle of many students. However, it would be wrong to see this as endemic. Alcohol is very much part of the student culture and always has been. Local alcohol purveyors know this and target students through promotions at pubs, clubs and halls of residence. Particular pub crawls are part of student mythology and become, in some cases, initiation ceremonies. Figures from the National Union of Students (NUS) indicate two further, more disturbing, facts: that the average student's weekly alcohol intake exceeds advisable unitary limits (21 for men and 14 for women), and that 10 per cent of students drink to dangerous levels (www.nus.online.advice). The UNITE Report shows that students spend on average almost £20 a week on alcohol. This average, however, hides three contrasting figures:

- A quarter of students do not spend anything on drink during a typical week. These are mostly non-white and international students, and those who are over 26 or live at home.
- Men spend almost twice as much as women on drink.
- A, B and C1 background students spend a third more than those from C2, D and E on drink.

There are similar figures on smoking. Just under a quarter of students spend money on tobacco, on average almost £16 a week. Those from a private school background tend to spend more. Universities and unions are very aware of the problems in these areas and are trying to promote a culture of a balanced lifestyle.

Patterns of behaviour on drugs and sex are of course very hard to estimate. Unofficial estimates are that over 50 per cent of students have at least tried soft drugs. Attitudes to sex are more complex than the usual student stereotype. While those at universities are at their most sexually active, the majority aim for marriage after university (64%).

Behind all this, the UNITE Report paints a more sober picture for the majority of students. Increasingly students see accommodation as more important than social life, and therefore a financial priority.

Different Experiences

In spite of the patterns revealed by these observations, the student experience is heavily dependent on the character of the institution. For many of the more recent universities and Further Education colleges there is little sense of any academic community. A high percentage of students live at home. The universities themselves are very functional and do not have space for the development of community. This contrasts with the college experience and the campus experience, each of which have a more traditional residential feel to community. Further Education colleges, on the other hand, can feel very much the centre of local community with many different links into that community. As such the experience for the student can be much more outward looking than at university, with a sense of the college servicing the community. In one sense this fits better with R. H. Tawney's vision of post-compulsory education in the service of the community, reaching back to the Workers Education Association (Robinson 1989).

Some Higher Education institutions have a very distinctive culture quite unlike that which you might expect of students. Agricultural colleges, for instance, may reflect the interests and concerns of the farming community and the Countryside Alliance.

Religious Student Narratives

Religions

The student culture has changed even more in terms of religion. Religious pluralism has exploded. Alongside the usual Christian societies are societies for all the major world religions, many with a national group to which they relate. The limits of religious identity are tested ever more by the presence of New Age groups and even by pagan and occult societies. This reached its height when in December 1994 Radio 1 announced that the University of Leeds had appointed a white witch as pagan chaplain. It was, of course, wrong. The Kabal student society had appointed the lady in question, and had every right to do so. The reaction from the press and some of the public, however, was very abrasive, with implications that the pagan chaplain would lead the students astray. This in turn held up the picture of students as a whole as vulnerable and unable to engage with different ideas. The Kabal student society stood firm on their decision. Their line was simple, 'If other religious groups have their chaplain then we want ours.' Behind this was the strong liberal line that students had the right to follow whatever faith they pleased. More than that there was the feeling that such groups wished to be recognized, not hidden away, as they so often are off campus. Along with this is a strong New Age stress on the anti-rational nature of spirituality. There are no rational grounds for discounting anyone's faith, other than harm to those involved. Such a level of tolerance questions all the old certainties. It also forces many traditional Christian groups to look carefully at their practices.

Behind the tolerance of faiths, however, is something even more vital, the public character of religious faiths. As Gilliat-Ray puts it, universities 'are a market place of religious ideas and beliefs, in microcosm, and the religious activity that takes place within them provide a unique context for exploring some of the collective dimensions of religion' (Gilliat-Ray 2000, 56). This is partly Bruce's point about universities being 'a charmed space' where persons have the chance to act as autonomous individuals (Bruce 1995, 30). It is also about an openness and directness of dialogue and debate, something not often replicated in the community.

Increasingly too, post-September 11th, there is a strong sense of the different religions finding it important to work together to respond to immediate crises. This can mean the different groups coming together, as Cohen (1995) puts it, to 'map out' the global religious and geopolitical issues onto 'the local terrain'. For all there is a marketplace this involves listening as much as proclaiming and responding to the needs of different faith groups. This stress on religious 'rights' at university is reinforced by the European Directives on religion or belief discrimination (*The Employment Equality (Religion or Belief) Regulations* SI 2003 No. 1660) which guard against discrimination or harassment on the grounds of religion. Even before that, universities had been very clear on the need to respect religious practices, not least when they clash with exams (Gilliat-Ray 2000).

Christian Student Groups

In one sense Christian students have benefited from the pluralist thinking. Student unions are happy to include many different Christian groups in their ranks, and very happy to be involved in working with interfaith and inter-Christian groups. One university has a Christian Medical Fellowship, Christian Union, Catholic society, SPEAK (a Christian justice group), Student Christian Movement, Anglican/Methodist society, Chinese Christian society and an Orthodox Christian society. This has led to an increased sense of a plurality at the heart of the Christian community, and an awareness of different viewpoints within different societies. One Christian Union of over 150 members includes 5 Roman Catholics. They like the biblical emphasis, and still go to Mass. The Christian Union is also increasingly aware of the debates within its ranks on 'post-evangelicalism', and is increasingly open to ethical debates on issues which up to ten years ago were perceived in hardline ways. Again it is not a matter of the CU retreating from a biblical position, but rather recognition that even biblically-based faith has many complexities to deal with.

This crossing of hitherto firm boundaries is also reflected in student approaches to denominations. The vast majority of students, Christian and non-Christian, have little or no understanding of Christian denominationalism. University has always been a place for Christian students to explore different approaches to the faith. One group of Christian students goes to a middle-of-the-road Methodist church next door to their halls of residence on Sunday morning and then to an evangelical Anglican church in the evening. There are groups who migrate en masse to the popular evangelical churches of the year, be they Baptist, Reformed Baptist, Anglican or Independent. With the increase in different student groups this takes on even more interesting mixes. One CU president uses a High Anglican church for her local congregation and members of an Anglican/Methodist society go to a monthly Orthodox chaplaincy service.

At the same time there are Christian students who do not want to be part of any student groups and who prefer to go to low-key or middle-of-the-road churches and best of all do not want to be noticed as students. There are also students who wish to go to local churches, but not to the regular services, i.e. where the older core group go.

Alongside the plurality of Christian life is also a shift in emphasis from the intellectual or doctrinal to the affective and participative approaches to faith. The Christian Union's often very cerebral concentration on the doctrinal meaning of Scripture has been replaced by more holistic practical and social concerns. The precise definition of the statement of faith is less important than the desire to pursue mission through friendship. As one UCCF (Universities and Colleges Christian Fellowship, the national body of the Christian Union) leader put it recently at a conference, this also reflects 'a culture increasingly dominated by symbol and image, with less prominence given to the written word'.

What does all this say about student religious culture? It points to a polyvocal Christian culture which as Meeks (1993) notes, writing of the second century, is nothing new. At the same time there are real changes, loosening of old boundaries and focusing more on practice and collaboration, and membership of different communities. Student experience is in any case a time of transition and this can tend to involve faith development.

Beyond and apart from the Church

Faith development may lead students to all kinds of different groups, often beyond the Church. Jamieson (2002) notes those younger Christians especially who purposely move away from formal church to marginal or liminal groups. The first of these largely define themselves in relation to what they have left, deconstructing the former views and beliefs. Liminal groups will tend to look forward, often developing their own patterns of worship. Many Christian student groups have taken on marginal and liminal characteristics, regardless of any national group aims. Some SCM groups, for instance, have been made up of a majority of students who do not have links to local churches and who find their spiritual identity in the groups. Students may also move into very different group experiences, such as Internet Communities. A good example of this is the Ship of Fools (www.ship-of-fools.com). This is advertised as a magazine of Christian unrest and has its own interactive community. It includes a wide range of Christians.

While the Christian Union remains quite healthy, the SCM groups are much less popular. There is much speculation as to why SCM has declined since its heyday in the 1960s and 1970s. It may be because some local groups do not have a clear positive identity, defining themselves negatively in relation to the CU or the traditional Church, or that they have not sustained links with either the local church or the national framework of their movement.

Alongside the Christian Union there is now a movement called Fusion (www.fusion.uk.com) which aims to build up cell groups, and ensure that these are networked to local churches.

Moving even further away from the traditional Church there is the affirmation of the spirituality of the person or group who are searching for their own life meaning in their particular context. This can be seen as part of the New Age. As Perry notes, for all the problems with New Age thinking 'it demonstrates a particularly useful attitude in understanding that life can be led as a self-reflective process of growth and transformation; and liberates spirituality from the confines of religious dogma and empowers direct personal experience' (Perry 1992, 36). It is about taking responsibility for spirituality, in the sense of ultimate life meaning.

This reaches a powerful expression in Douglas Coupland's *Generation X* (1992). Coupland's concept is contentious. It focuses on the generation between the 1960s and 1980s in America, and makes several generalizations about this. For all the problems in doing that he does point to a section of society which has grown up disengaged from traditional sources of meaning, lacking in a sense of meaning, and searching for meaning in their particular context (Lynch 2002). University life fosters such an attitude. The curriculum often critiques traditional sources of meaning, and there are many who are genuinely searching for meaning.

Lynch (2002) suggests in all this that the search for meaning can be related to popular culture, exemplified in the club scene. The club scene is, in every sense, a dark area for the Christian Church. For many it is associated with a hedonistic lifestyle and the world of drugs. There is no denying the problems that surround this culture, and the way in which the club experience can be abused. However, once again, this scene is far more complex than at first sight. In one large city every Tuesday evening (student night) some 4,000 students regularly go through just one club. Lynch (2002) points to the similarities between the experience of club dancing and religious and meditative experiences. Many club-goers themselves see the experience of dancing, and the associated altered state of consciousness, as a spiritual experience, in which the affective and somatic aspects of the person are affirmed. Once again the significance of such experience can be debated, but what cannot be denied is the scale of such a culture and that many students are very much a part of this and find important meaning at affective and somatic levels.

Balancing this, some students explore life meaning through altruistic activities. Some 7 per cent of students are actively involved in charity work of some kind (UNITE 2003). A quarter of students in the UNITE Report express a desire to get involved in such work when study permits.

Conclusion

This all too brief overview of student culture demonstrates that there is no single or simple student culture. Instead, there are many voices expressing different cultural perspectives, some of which are well established and others which are not. Some of these embody closed cultures, such as the utilitarian focus on a degree and work. Others express open culture and the capacity for dialogue, such as some religious groups and generation X. Others are a mixture, or haven't really thought through what culture they do express. This means different cultures will have different emphases depending upon their local context. It is partly the task of the chaplain to begin to understand all these voices, how they come together and how they relate.

Despite the essential diversity, overall trends can be traced across the sector, from the experience of mass education to the growth of a more consumerist ethos. As these trends occur they are, as we shall see, invariably ambiguous, with exciting possibilities and problems. And they set up several major challenges to the Church and any chaplaincy presence:

- How should the Church relate to a culture of liberal tolerance? If all views are as good as the next how can the chaplain begin to enable spiritual and ethical challenge?
- How can the Church relate to the very different elements which work against community or which actually explore very different kinds of community? One implication of mass education is that there is simply not the time and space for the provision of developing chaplaincy programmes. Even if there is, different people may be attending each week. Other areas may provide important and challenging possibilities for communities in transition, with spiritualities that are unlike any the Church is used to.

Underlying all of these different communities and changes are groups, movements and individuals who are in transition, between faith stages, different groups, life stages and so on. And this perhaps poses the major question of any practical theology of chaplaincy, not simply how we engage with another community, but how we engage with a sector of many communities in transition. None of this can be placed into the category of traditional youth work, and getting a handle on this diversity demands the foundation of a practical theology of chaplaincy.

Before that, however, we need to address the practical foundations of how a chaplaincy can be established.

References

Baldwin, J., 'Personal Development Planning', *Times Higher Education Supplement*, 23 May 2003, L5.

Barnett, R., 'Supercomplexity and the Curriculum', *Studies in Higher Education* 25 (3), 2000, pp. 255–65.

Baudrillard, J., *Simulations*, Semiotext, New York, 1983.

Bruce, S., *Religion in Modern Britain*, Oxford University Press, Oxford, 1995.

Brueggemann, W., *Theology of the Old Testament*, Abingdon, Nashville, 1997.

Cohen, P., 'The Crisis of the Western University', in Cohen, P. (ed.), *For a Multicultural University,* New Ethnicities Unit: University of East London, working paper no.3, 1995, pp. 1–7.

Connor, S., *The Post Modern Culture*, Blackwell, Oxford, 1989.

Coupland, D., *Generation X*, Abacus, London, 1992.

Gilliat-Ray, S., *Religion in Higher Education*, Ashgate, Aldershot, 2000.

Jamieson, A., *A Churchless Faith*, SPCK, London, 2002.

Lynch, G., *After Religion*, DLT, London, 2002.

Lyotard, J-F., *The Postmodern Condition,* Manchester University Press, Manchester, 1979.

Meeks, W., *The Origins of Christian Morality*, Yale University Press, New Haven, 1993.

Perry, M., *Gods Within*, SPCK, London, 1992.

Perry, M., 'Idealism and Drift', in Watt, J. (ed.), *The Church, Medicine and the New Age*, The Churches' Council for Health and Healing, London, 1995.

Reader J., *Beyond All Reason*, Aureus, Cardiff, 1997.

Robinson, S., 'R. H. Tawney's Equality: A Theological and Ethical Analysis', unpublished PhD thesis, University of Edinburgh, 1989.

Thomas, L., *Widening participation, increasing wastage? Issues of student retention,* Institute for Access Studies, Staffordshire University, 2002.

UNITE, 'Student Living Report', www.unite-group.co.uk, 2003.

2

Practical Foundations

The Anglican Bishop of Plumpton decided that it would be a good idea to set up a chaplaincy in the newly formed University of Plumpton. Being a modern university the right place for chaplaincy seemed to be in student services, and discussions were set up with the student services manager. The manager was an enthusiastic Christian, keen to develop a professional approach to student services, including a chaplaincy. The agreement was made between bishop and university and some space was provided for the chaplain. The assumption was made that the key chaplain would be Anglican. At the same time a small ecumenical team was developing, which was very keen to share tasks and space.

The team stayed together for three years and when the Anglican left another Anglican was appointed as lead chaplain. However, within a year, major problems began to emerge. The team felt that it was not clear about its objectives and that the Anglican was taking too much responsibility. The student services manager was becoming increasingly unsure about the role of chaplaincy. He called in the lead chaplain and asked why he was not ensuring that pastoral cover was being provided in the office or in the foyer of the main building, as had been initially agreed. The chaplain's response was that the other members of the team did not see the point of doing this, and so he was finding it hard to maintain such a service. The manager did not see why there should be change in service, especially without consulting him. He was also concerned about the way in which the team seemed to be responding to the lead chaplain. As a result he contacted the bishop to see if he could sort out the situation. The bishop however felt powerless because there was an ecumenical agreement which meant that it should be sorted out within the local ecumenical sponsoring body. This body, however, did not have any clear mechanism for working such a problem through. While it was trying to work that out, through the mechanism of a review, the strain became too much for the lead chaplain and he resigned.

Horror stories like this one have happened in the not-too-distant past, and analyzing it could keep one busy for some time. The key stakeholders in this case were the university, the Anglican bishop, the ecumenical sponsoring body and the ecumenical team.

The bishop had, with the best of intentions, set up a potentially creative relationship with the university but not bothered to consult other stakeholders. This is not just an Anglican problem. When it comes to making appointments of chaplains, many chaplaincies can point to lack of awareness in all denominations.

In turn the ecumenical team was not clear about what was going on. The institution seemed at all points to relate to the bishop rather than them or the ecumenical sponsoring group. They did not feel that the second 'lead chaplain' was actually enabling them to develop as a team. In turn the head of student services felt that there was loss of discipline in the team.

This case highlights some of the major issues in setting up an HE chaplaincy. For healthcare, prison or forces chaplaincy the lines of communication and management are clear. These various bodies give chaplains contracts and there have been various attempts to ensure clarity of expectations (Robinson, Kendrick and Brown 2003). Despite the majority of chaplains in these areas being ordained they are not formally or primarily accountable to the local church.

In Higher Education, Oxbridge colleges, some Scottish universities and some modern universities, such as Sheffield Hallam, provide contracts for their chaplains, but these are the exception. In these cases the institutional chaplain then becomes responsible for co-ordinating work with denominational chaplains and for developing relationships with the local church.

However, as the case above underlines, the Church and the university can be very unclear about how chaplains relate to each other. Any mechanism for management needs to be carefully worked out in context. That context may reveal very different perceptions and ways of dealing with chaplaincies. The more modern universities see them as a managed part of the student support services. Others see them as quite apart from such a management structure. Others are uneasy about the very idea of religious organizations operating on campus where student autonomy is paramount. Others have some sense of student and staff religious rights and see chaplaincy in this light. Universities have different ways of recognizing the chaplain, from recognizing each chaplain through a formal Senate committee, to recognizing the team, who are then responsible, with church and university, for appointments (Gilliat-Ray 2000, 76–8).

Often the local church is not clear about roles, simply assuming a model such as the chaplain working exclusively with denominational students. Questions abound. Which bit of the local church should the chaplain fit into? How far is the chaplaincy part of the strategy of the local church? Who should the chaplain report to?

The case above never even began to address these issues, leading to a breakdown in pastoral relations between the churches, within the team and between the church and the university. It almost led to the withdrawal of the service.

For the majority of chaplaincies then careful attention is needed in three areas:

- Relations between the chaplaincy and the churches.
- Relations within the team.
- Relations to the academic institution.

There are many ways of firming up these relationships, all of which demand close attention to the local situation and careful negotiation. What follows are simply a number of different approaches which work.

The Church

The first step is to decide how the work of chaplaincy is to be organized. It is clear that given the size of modern universities it is important for chaplains of all denominations to work together in an ecumenical team in the area of pastoral care and mission, and in some way in worship. Such a team can:

- Embody the unity of the Church.
- Increase the resources on offer enabling the chaplaincy to do much more. It is essentially about collaborative ministry.
- Provide a single point of initial contact for the vast majority of students who, as noted above, are unaware of any denominational differences.

• Embody and sustain inclusive mission, open to all (Avis 1999).

These points might be embodied in a local ecumenical project, especially if there is a building involved. This would be brokered by the local ecumenical officer. Another way forward is through a covenant between the leaders, committing themselves to this as part of their joint strategy of mission and outreach. An example of such a covenant is:

Concerning provision of Christian Chaplaincy in The University of . . .

WE, THE UNDERSIGNED, BELIEVE that the ministry of Chaplains in The University of ... is a critical part of the mission of the Church.

WE ARE THANKFUL that those who have this particular responsibility and have been appointed by us severally have agreed to plan to act together, sharing insights and resources, and we recognise that this has made more effective the work of Chaplaincy.

WE AFFIRM the commitment and collaboration which already exists.

WE COMMIT ourselves to support, develop and encourage the work of Chaplaincy in the University.

WE UNDERTAKE
• to confer with one another, especially about appointments
• to consider carefully how we may share available resources

WE CALL UPON those whom we appoint to pray, to plan, to work and to grow together for the building up of God's kingdom.

WE COMMEND the procedures formulated by the Chaplaincy and attached hereto.

WE ENTRUST the four-yearly review of this Chaplaincy to the . . . Ecumenical Council.

WE INVITE other member denominations of the Council of Churches for Britain and Ireland to join us in this commitment to Chaplaincy in . . .

Signed . . . Church leaders.

Date:

This example was built on an initial personal covenant between the members of the chaplaincy team. The limitation of the personal covenant is that it does not enable overall consistency of team relationships. The leaders' covenant establishes a clear way of working together. It accepts that operational decision about priorities will be taken in the team and they will be reflected on in the ecumenical review. Hence, it gives space for the team to develop its operation and ensures that it is accountable.

If the practical operation of chaplaincy is based in the ecumenical agreement it is important for the denominational organizations to be at one with this. This means each denomination signing up to the mission statement, means of planning, review and so on. To have a separate line management and accountability to the denomination runs the danger of a conflict of accountability and a loss of focus. The individual chaplain should nonetheless ensure that reports do go to the appropriate denominational body, so that any question can be raised. Such a body should be clear where HE chaplaincy fits in to the mission strategy of the particular church, and why it is best to pursue this as an ecumenical team.

Denominations can also supply a support group, allowing the chaplain in question the space to share his work, think through any particular issues and identify any issues that might need to be addressed by the ecumenical leaders. In any case if the practice of chaplaincy is ecumenical it is perfectly possible for the any key denominational representative or line manager to be part of the ecumenical steering group or council. The key principle is to provide practice-centred support and management from the churches, which backs up the team which is effecting the mission of chaplaincy.

It is worthwhile thinking carefully what the best denominational home is for chaplaincy. Some Anglican dioceses, for instance, place it in the board of education, mirroring the approach the national Board of Education. Some question this, not least because the stress on church schools can tend to be neither ecumenical nor mission-oriented. On the other hand, provided the ecumenical framework is in place, such a board could support an overview which takes in HE, FE and primary and secondary education. There could be many overlaps in mission.

A separate but related issue is how the chaplaincy might relate to the local churches. Some denominations argue that it is important to fit into the mission strategy of the local area organization. This is problematic, given that institutions are often on very different campuses, some outside the 'local area', and that it can take the focus away from ecumenical working. Hence, unless the chaplaincy is denominational it is better to relate to local churches through networking than management.

The Team

Katzenbach and Smith (1993) usefully distinguish a team from a group. Teams involve:

- A common purpose, with agreed performance goals.
- A common approach to working.
- Disciplined action.
- A high level of interdependency.
- Complementary skills.
- Mutual accountability.

The first of these demands the development of a clear mission statement that can be agreed upon by all stakeholders. The following is an example of such a statement.

Christian Chaplains' Mission Statement

The Chaplains are committed to working together ecumenically in order to:

- Offer spiritual and pastoral care to all members of the university.
- Nurture spiritual growth through the provision of opportunities for worship, prayer, study, and the development of faith communities.
- Foster discussion and action on social justice, ethical and spiritual issues.
- Help to build a sense of community within the university and to build appropriate links within the university and between the university and the churches and other faiths.

The Chaplain's model of practice is based on mutual reflection, openness, exploration and prayer.

Broadly speaking this sets out a mission based upon pastoral work, worship, prophecy and networking. It is intentionally broad so that all stakeholders can feel comfortable with it. Hence it does not use mission language that could be perceived as aggressive or assertive. Whatever the final statement, it should be agreed by all the team, the different denominations and the university. This statement also says something about the approach to team working. This, however, needs to be spelt out in clear procedures such as those in the following example.

PROCEDURES FOR WORKING IN PARTNERSHIP IN CHAPLAINCY IN THE UNIVERSITY OF . . .

Introduction

The Chaplaincy team (hereafter referred to as 'team') includes chaplains appointed by churches participating in the . . . Ecumenical Council (EC). They are full-time/part-time, paid/unpaid, male/female, lay/ordained.

Operational matters

1. The team operates as one, with different operational centres.
2. The team relates to the institution through a Service Level Agreement.
3. The team meets fortnightly during term time.
4. There is one coordinator whose task is to relate closely to the institution and to ensure that team activities in that institution are coordinated, making the most of the team's resources.
5. The coordinator and the team administrative officer meet in alternate weeks to plan the agenda for the team meeting and to deal with any outstanding business.
6. The coordinator is agreed on by the team for a 3 year period.
7. There is an annual residential meeting of the team for planning purposes.

8. The team holds an annual general meeting at which the audited accounts are received.
9. The team aims to support each other pastorally. In the event of a serious pastoral problem the coordinators will work closely with the denomination in question.
10. Complaints procedure: As per University Student Handbook.
11. Team members are subject to the normal discipline of their denominations.

Appointments

1. Chaplains are appointed by the faith communities of which they are part. It is agreed by all parties that prior consultation with the team and with the University should occur, and is an essential part of the appointment process.
2. The Chaplaincy Advisory Council having representation from all these bodies has the responsibility of coordinating this process of consultation.
3. The University is only able to accept a new appointment after adequate consultation has taken place.

Finance

Each appointing body is responsible for the pay and housing of their chaplain(s), where appropriate, and also contributes to the operational costs of the team. The balance of the operational costs is provided through the Service Level Agreements.

Relationships with other Faiths

The team aims to work closely with representatives of other faiths in the University, encouraging both pastoral coordination and interfaith dialogue.

Review

The team's operation is reviewed every five years, with reference to the mission statement. This will be facilitated by the Chaplaincy Advisory Council.

The engine room for such an agreement is a combination of an annual review and planning away days. Over two days the previous year's work is reviewed, priorities re-examined and objectives set out for the year to come. The objectives may involve maintenance of regular activities or new projects. These may involve projects such as worship, or outreach, making links or collaborating with different areas and departments on campus. One or more members of the team will be responsible for each objective, and will report back to team meetings on their progress. Mutual accountability is thereby part of the whole process, based on agreed objectives and responsibilities.

The regular team meetings during the semester should focus first on feedback from the chaplains both about projects and intelligence. For instance the chaplain responsible for liaising with the student union can report back on any issues being raised there or on ongoing projects. The second focus of the meeting could be mutual support. Some teams have found prayer and contextual Bible study before the meeting to be a good basis for this support, as well as important for rigorous theological reflection. Third, these meetings will also have to deal with any major issues emerging during the year.

The role of the co-ordinator of any chaplaincy team should be worked on and agreed by all stakeholders. Broadly, however, it should include co-ordination with the university in question and co-ordination of the team's efforts. The first involves what the university sees as the head of department role. This involves networking with other heads of departments, both academic and support services, and frequent consultation with the university management heads, including the vice-chancellor. The second, at its simplest, involves ensuring that objectives are agreed and that the team fulfils its objectives. Where any team member is finding difficulty the co-ordinator should help them identify the problem and work through it. There is therefore a clear management function in this position though not necessarily a directive or prescriptive one.

Chaplaincy Council

A chaplaincy council of some form is an important element in any constitution. There are examples of universities with different councils, such as for building as well as team operation. This can easily lead to confusion. There are councils which are simply drawn from church representatives. This does not enable real transparency and feedback from all the different groups. Hence, a council is best when it includes representatives from all stakeholders, academic institution and churches. It provides a point of accountability. It can also provide a forum for consultation about appointments. The chair can consult with the appointing denomination and the academic institution in question can allow the issue of appointments and therefore recognition of the chaplain to be given to the council. Where the appointment is made by the institution the council can still act as facilitator of the process.

The council does not actually manage the team but does have a role similar to the board of a company. Part of the constitution of such a council is shown below.

The University of . . . Chaplaincy Advisory Council Constitution (Draft 2)

1. Aims

The Chaplaincy Advisory Council exists to encourage and support the work of the Ecumenical Team of Christian Chaplains in the University of . . .

The Council does this by:

  i. Receiving reports on the work of the Chaplaincy Team in each institution
 ii. Giving reflective comment on planning and practice
iii. Raising awareness in the churches and the universities of the value and role of Chaplaincy
 iv. Coordinating the consultation process in regard to appointments
  v. Receiving audited accounts annually on behalf of stakeholders, after they have been agreed by the Chaplaincy Team
 vi. Negotiating continued financial support with universities and churches

2. Membership

Churches: eight representatives.
Each of the . . . denominations that sponsor chaplains appoint one representative. Three of these representatives are also members of the . . . Ecumenical Council.

Four representatives of the university appointed by:
The Vice-chancellor, the Student Union, the Christian Student Forum, and the staff group.
Three representatives from the Chaplaincy team, including the coordinator and administrator.

All members share responsibility for the fulfilment of the Council's aims (see 1).

Members normally serve for three years, with the possibility of being appointed for a second term of three years.

3. Reporting Responsibility

The Council reports to Ecumenical Sponsoring Group, to the supporting denominations and to the universities through the representative members, as necessary.

Team Issues

Boundaries

There are broadly two major boundary issues. The first is that of the boundary between the church and the university and this can be handled through the work of the team and the council. The second is the boundary of the team itself. Can any groups join the team? It is certain that many may see it in their interests to be part of it. In Christian terms the easiest criteria are whether the group who wants to be involved in the team can actually agree to the mission statement and can honestly work together with the different members of the team. Most often use of these criteria leads to self-exclusion. One team had two representatives of the American Southern Baptists apply to become members of the team, and eventually they decided they simply could not honestly be part of the team. Other teams have been able to accommodate such diverse groups as the

Orthodox Church and the Chinese Christian Church by using the same criteria.

Appointment Procedures

These should reflect the ecumenical framework. Once the different parties have been consulted, not least the team about its needs, then the best solution is to have an appointing committee focused around the chaplaincy committee. Whilst this may not be necessary for part-time chaplains, there should still be consultation between the team and the appointing church. The issue of job description will be returned to in Chapter 11.

All the major churches have national HE and FE chaplaincy advisors, and it is important to consult them about appointments, and possibly to have them involved in the appointing committee.

Full- or Part-time

Teams tend to have a mixture of full- and part-time chaplains. The team framework, with planning and co-ordination, enables part-timers both to be fully part of the setting of objectives and to take responsibility for particular areas of chaplaincy. A part-timer with experience in business, for instance, can take on the development of links with a business school or the Centre for Business and Professional Ethics. For the part-timer any role would be negotiated with the team, based on skills, team need and shared objectives. The team context of chaplaincy means that there can be a mixture of ordained and lay members. The greater part of the chaplaincy role does not require an ordained person.

Team Balance and Complementary Skills and Interests

If the team is operating on agreed objectives and in the light of clear expectations with the university then it is important to try to maintain team balance. This may include chaplains who have strong experience in teaching, pastoral work, administration, working with international students and so on. Any of these might be included in the recruitment criteria as desirable. Clearly the constraints of any appointing church may make this difficult. If that is not possible then it is important to plan team training to take these needs into account. One example of this is for the team to provide the finances for one of the members to be trained in, for instance, international student work or pastoral counselling. Where a team loses a teacher, for instance, it may be possible to bring in a replacement from outside the team, funded by the service level agreement (SLA). Where possible there should also be balance of gender and age. Chaplaincy assistants, usually recent graduates, can help meet the latter.

Training

In-house training for chaplains involves three areas that the team can enable:

- Information. This is about the various different legislation and guidelines.
- Pastoral and outreach training for the whole team (see Chapter 6).
- Training identified for particular members to ensure that objectives can be fulfilled.

Some training can be supplied by the academic institution. It can also be provided through national chaplaincy conferences or regional training schemes, where they are in operation.

Training for teamwork is also important. Professional Development Units are offered by some university departments, enabling team development over two years leading to accreditation for the whole team. Such units enable reflective practice focusing on the service provided by chaplaincy for students and staff, and how it can be improved.

One Team or Two

In large cities there is increasingly the question of how teams in different universities work together. At one point it was argued that the differences between universities are such that it is important to have separate teams who can come together when discussing matters of common concern. In practice, this is not always the best option for several reasons:

- Many denominations appoint chaplains to the HE and FE institutions in one city.

- Many such institutions are geographically close.
- Having one overall team with different operational centres can ensure economy of scale, good inter-campus creativity, cross-fertilization, and best use of resources, material and human. If one university has little possibility of traditional community building, for instance, it would make little sense not to use someone working largely in another campus who is experienced in curriculum involvement. Equally, if one team member has a good relationship with engineering in one university it might make sense for them to link to design and building in another.

This arrangement would simply be written into the team's constitution, with, for instance, two co-ordinators ensuring that the particular needs of each institution are met. For many modern universities the problem of different operational centres is already very much an issue, with some having as many as ten different sites. Again this is where co-ordination of part-time team members becomes very important, giving them responsibility for different sites.

This also raises the question of how HE and FE chaplains relate. With the greater closeness of the two sectors it might make sense for them to work together in any local area.

Reviews

The process of evaluation of chaplaincy work is in one sense ongoing. This is part of the role of the review and planning days and of the council. There may be other mechanisms of feedback. One good example is a student well-being survey at the University of Leeds. This survey is run three times a year to get a sense of the level of well-being among students. In one of these questionnaires students are asked to assess the support given by campus agencies, including the chaplaincy. Though a rough indicator, it does enable external feedback to the chaplains.

The regular review of operation and teamwork by the sponsoring body should be part of any ecumenical agreement. Broad suggestions for such a review include:

- Constituency might be one external consultant, usually a chaplain, and two nominees of the council – representing university and church.

- The task of the review group should centre on aims, objectives and practice, reflecting back on how the review group perceives these.
- This can be seen as part of the learning process of the team. Hence it should not be judgemental but rather reflective, enabling the team and council both to affirm the work being done and to see where there are conflicts, contradictions and inconsistencies in operation and team relationships. The team and chaplaincy council and sponsoring body should then have to take responsibility for dealing with these things.
- The review group should hear views from all 'stakeholders', including students and institution, and as a far as possible all submissions should be open.

Reviews by denominations will differ somewhat, not least because they will often be assessing whether the post should be kept. Such reviews will need to give attention to the practical focus of the team, and might consider:

- The use of an external consultant, possibly the national advisor.
- Review of the area or diocesan mission strategy to see how chaplaincy is involved in this.
- Any obligations beyond the diocese or local area, for instance, to national mission strategy, to other areas whose members may be students, or to ecumenical partners.
- An ecumenical member of the panel.

Once more it is critical that this should be a transparent process, not least because of the ecumenical connections.

Chalk and Cheese

The idea of developing teamwork in a church organization seems, on the face of it, to be doomed before it starts. There are inevitably too many different traditions, with different theological, ecclesiological and pastoral approaches.

However, first, it is important to have different traditions within the team, so that respectful listening and effective collaboration can be modelled to the different traditions on campus. Second, differences can be worked through very effectively. In worship, for instance, it is possible to have different services, or to have a central worship time, at which the different traditions contribute on a rota basis.

In terms of pastoral care, pastoral counselling can sit side by side with laying on of hands, provided a clear operational method is established, e.g. including healing as part of the eucharist, or developing an agreed protocol for when healing rituals might be appropriate.

Appraisal

Denominations will tend to be responsible for individual appraisals, though they could include an ecumenical dimension.

The Academic Institution

Clarifying the relationship of the chaplain or chaplaincy to the university is the final step. Where a chaplain is employed by the university this will involve a time-limited personal contract. This should include in it how the lead chaplain is to relate to the Christian denominations and other faiths, and a clear job description.

Most chaplaincy members are employed by their local churches, and will need to negotiate some other kind of relationship with the university. The most effective way is through a contract between the team and the institution, a form of services level agreement (SLA). The agreement will set down what services the team will provide to the university, and what the university will give in return, in terms of finances or other resources to support the service. The advantage of the SLA is that it ensures precise expectations without taking away from the autonomy of the chaplaincy team. Hence, the team would not be 'controlled' by a student services manager. A services level agreement will typically articulate:

- The purpose, an example of which is shown below.
- Content of the services.
- Support structures including reference to any chaplaincy council.
- Appointment procedures.
- The university's recognition of the chaplains as associate staff in some form.

- Means of reporting and review.
- Agreed services in detail.
- Agreed renumeration for the services, and note of which parties are responsible for salaries/stipends and housing.

A SERVICES LEVEL AGREEMENT
Between . . . University and the . . . Ecumenical Chaplaincy Team

PURPOSE OF THIS AGREEMENT

. . . University recognizes and affirms the value of the faith traditions of its staff and students and seeks to work in partnership with faith communities to offer support and care for the University community. To this end the University currently recognizes an Islamic advisor, a Jewish Chaplain and an ecumenical Chaplaincy Team of Christian Chaplains, who work under the auspices of the . . . Ecumenical Council (EC). The University will continue to seek representatives from other faith traditions that are represented in the University.

The faith communities recognize the value of Higher Education as something that contributes both to self-development and the development of communities. The faith communities also recognize the role . . . University plays in . . . and the wider region. Historically this recognition has had practical expression in the commitment by some faith communities to work in partnership with the University by designating Chaplains and supporting them financially. These Chaplains are independent of the University but work within University guidelines and policies. They also work together while recognizing and respecting diverse traditions.

The ecumenical Chaplaincy Team of Christian Chaplains provides services that are available to all members of the University.

This effective partnership has been established over many years. The purpose of this agreement is to build on and develop

ership by identifying the services provided by the
and the support provided by the University.

The precise services offered by the chaplaincy will depend upon
detailed negotiation with the university in question, taking account
of the local context, both at the university and in the church. Some
teams may not be in a position to provide teaching. In some secular
universities, for instance, it may be deemed unacceptable to include
reference to worship, other than in a pastoral context, in an SLA. In
such a case, because the chaplaincy remains an autonomous service
provider it would simply continue to provide worship outside the
SLA. One comprehensive list of services is set out by one chaplaincy
below:

PROVISION OF SERVICES

As the following makes clear, Chaplaincy is positioned within
Student Services but its remit and its work extends beyond it.

1. Pastoral care

a) Personal support to students and staff
  - Being available at set times for part of each weekday in
    term time
  - Providing an on call service out of hours and in vacations
  - Providing hospitality to groups and individuals as
    appropriate
  - Making and receiving referrals to and from other services

b) Crisis and bereavement care in line with university
   procedures
  - Offering support
  - Making home visits when appropriate
  - Making hospital visits when requested
  - Arranging special services when requested
  - Participating in Crisis Management Group
  - Liaising with the other faith advisors where required

c) International Student care and support
(The team has a member with special responsibility for this in
addition to it being a general responsibility of all Chaplains)
  - All services listed under 1 a)

- Convening and servicing the University group of those working with International Students
- Helping to promote and lead International Student Club
- Leading study and discussion groups as requested
- Offering hospitality
- Organizing visits
- Assisting International Students' Adviser as and when requested
- Being alert to particular needs arising from events in countries from which students come and offering support at these times

2. Spirituality

a) Inter-faith work
   - Liaising between faith groups and fostering mutual respect and understanding
   - Maintaining good communications between faith representatives
   - Providing information about all faith communities as needed
   - Organizing opportunities for discussions and joint action

b) Worship and other events
   - Providing regular opportunities for Christian worship, study and prayer
   - Organizing religious services to mark special events
   - Providing opportunities for silence, space, reflection

c) Spiritual Development
   - Accompanying those who are exploring questions of faith and spirituality
   - Giving informal support to student societies
   - Responding to requests to be involved in teaching or development of course materials
   - Advising staff if concerns arise around 'cult' activities

3. Ethics

   - Participating in debate about values in Higher Education
   - Participating in work of University Ethics Committee

- Contributing to discussion of ethical and social justice issues in a variety of forums
- Responding to requests to be involved in teaching or development of course materials
- Supervising research students if/when requested
- Arranging occasional lectures

4. Community Building

- Developing opportunities for cross-Faculty networking
- Offering occasional workshops through Staff Development programme
- Strengthening public awareness of the University in local faith communities and vice versa.

SLAs can be regularly reviewed and refreshed, and form the basis for continual reflection on value and purpose for all parties. There was a point when it was thought that such contracts were not possible. Secular universities would not seek to contract with religious organizations, and religious organizations would not want to be tied down to secular aims. SLAs or similar contracts give the means of bridging that gap, ensuring the autonomy of the team, clear expectations for the university, and a framework for articulation of spiritual and pastoral care on campus. They can thus be the basis for a mutual and creative relationship. The very process of negotiating an SLA might take up to a year, and can develop trust between the chaplaincy and the academic institution.

The SLA can be made between a denominational team and the institution where there is no possibility of an ecumenical team. It can also be made on the basis of an interfaith team. However, the nature of an interfaith team needs to be thought through carefully. A great number of the services provided above go well beyond the provision of a simple faith service, i.e. something provided for a particular faith group. Crisis and bereavement work, for instance, is open to all students and involves spirituality much broader than any one faith. Moreover, broader spiritual care and that of particular faiths needs to be co-ordinated. For the most part non-Christian faiths do not see themselves in such a role. It is important to note that any renumeration from the academic institution is based on this broader role. The role in this case parallels that of the institutional chaplain, i.e. one paid by the university. Gilliat-Ray (2000, 72) mischaracterizes this situation when she infers that Christian chaplaincies paid by the university simply use the money for their own community and worship events.

Conclusion

This chapter has set out different ways of establishing relationships between church and academic institutions. For these to be effective, in addition to structure, there needs to be good timing. The review and planning of the team needs to be co-ordinated with the chaplaincy council. Reporting to the council at the end of the year should be coordinated with reporting to university committees and any denominational groups. Best of all, all should receive the same report, so that all stakeholders are clear about progress and how planning is being managed. It is a good example of collaborative work occurring on several levels. The organization should enable the team to continue to develop and ensure that the aims and interests of both major parties, the church and the university are being addressed.

Discussion of these aims, however, takes us into what the underlying practical theology of chaplaincy might be.

References

Avis, P., 'Towards a theology of sector ministry', in Legood, G. (ed.) *Chaplaincy*, Cassell, London, 1999, pp. 3–14.

Gilliat-Ray, S., *Religion in Higher Education*, Ashgate, Aldershot, 2000.

Katzenbach, J. R. and Smith, D.K., *The Wisdom of Teams*, Harper Business, New York, 1993.

Robinson, S., Kendrick, K. and Brown, A., *Spirituality and the Practice of Healthcare*, Palgrave Macmillan, Basingstoke, 2003.

3

Singing the Lord's Song:
A Practical Theology of Chaplaincy

Every community should have a body of bridge-builders, pontifices, a very good name, for the bridge builder is the real priest. These are the beavers of society, unobtrusive gentle animals, yet with sharp teeth and bright eyes, eyes to see where piles must be driven, what stout timbers must be felled. Where the bars to bind and fasten must be set, teeth to cut down obstructions and bite them into place.

(Tawney 1970)

We left chaplaincy in Chapter 1 facing an explosion in HE and trying to work out how to relate to the many different stake-holders:

- The increasingly professionalized, specialist and centralized student support services.
- The postmodern and liberal culture of this student world.
- The increasingly customer driven approach of the institution.
- The increasing attempts to widen participation but at the same time to work from limited resources.

This is indeed a strange and different land in which to sing the Lord's Song. In the light of this, this chapter will first examine more closely and critique the models of chaplaincy that have been prac-tised over the past 50 years. It will then draw out a broad practical theology of chaplaincy.

Models of HE Chaplaincy

Collegiate Model

The collegiate model (Wright 1985) is most obviously seen in universities and colleges with religious origins. With the breakdown of Anglican domination, chaplains developed naturally in a context where there were resources, including a chapel, and where it was accepted that all would share basic belief systems and values. Today the dean and/or chaplain have a position often at the centre of the college, with the task of maintaining the chapel and worship, and in many cases the highest profile pastoral role for a relatively small number of students and staff. The college is the chaplain's natural environment as many chaplains will also have academic expertise. It is assumed that the Church has every right to be at the centre of this activity.

Of course, it is never as simple as that. Colleges today, despite their size, are still complex organizations, under the same pressures as the rest of Higher Education. As such, in practice they have many different views about chaplaincy and the Church. The collegiate model never really had to justify itself or to articulate an underlying theology, but now some colleges are even seeking to cut back on chaplaincy provision.

The Church Model

This focuses less on the Higher Education community and more on the gathered congregation. In this the chaplain is seen as a extension of the Church, much like a parish priest or local minister, whose task it is to service the church community and then reach out. This is often, though not exclusively, denominational, with success focused on developing the worshipping community. This model does recognize a difference between the Church and the surrounding community, and looks to maintain that Church for the future, through the developing of church leaders, lay and ordained. Hence, the task of the chaplain has often been connected to fostering vocations, especially in the narrow sense of ordination.

This model was associated with post-1945 history and the increase in campus universities, where no chaplaincy provision was offered by the universities and the gathered congregation was seen as the key to relating to the institution.

The Liberationist Model

The 1960s were a time of change and questioning. Anxiety and anger were expressed about oppressive power structures, exemplified by the Vietnam protests. With this emerged in the UK, albeit briefly, a model of chaplaincy as prophetic and liberationist, radical in theology and left wing in politics (Robinson and Benwell 2000). The chaplain would identify with these protests and speak out against oppressive power structures in the university and beyond. Hence, chaplains joined students in sit-ins and protests. This was chaplaincy with an attitude and a cause, not always shared by the majority of the Church.

The Waterloo Model

With the new universities and polytechnics, and with no real sense of community, different attempts arose to relate to the university – none of which were exclusive.

These were attempts to be seen to be visible and so to set up relationships in a community which Wright (1985) compares to Waterloo Station. People are continually on the move, with no time to engage, even if there were a place to invite them to. This model relies on building up relationships and is closely related to the 'loitering with intent' model. In this the chaplain would be seen walking the corridors, having meals in the refectories and so on. The chaplain's presence was a sign of the Church's concern, leading to conversations, friendships, pastoral care, and building up networks. The 'intent' was simply to engage and see what might follow.

The Student Services Model

This is a model increasingly being explored by the most recent universities in which the university has a clearer say about the function of chaplaincy. It is partly a function of management style, which wants all services to be managed. It includes the articulation of objectives, and the management of limited resources. At least two universities pay for their own chaplain on this basis. Several others look to locate chaplaincy as part of the student services, under the student services manager. Such a model sees the chaplain as directly accountable to the university, and as primarily a pastoral resource.

This does not take away from the religious functions of the chaplain, but does increasingly look to chaplaincy as a customer-oriented organization.

Criticism of the Models

None of these models are adequate of themselves. The strength of the first model is that the chaplain has a very clear role and is seen as an integral part of the community. In practice too this collegiate approach has a relatively small number of students and staff for the chaplain to relate to. However, it is not adequate precisely because the postmodern campus is massively different, as indeed is the post Christian experience. The model assumes that there is no 'other' to engage with – since the entire community shares the same values. In practice, however, many chaplains have no official place within the institution, and are not seen or understood by the majority of students or staff. In such a context the Christian chaplain takes her place alongside different faiths, and can claim no privilege in terms of power or narrative significance.

The second model provides a secure and stable spiritual community for students and staff alike. Many students do need such a community, often in the short term. The deficiency of this model, however, is of narrowing the focus of chaplaincy, especially to the development of a denominational community, and of losing awareness of the needs of the wider HE communities. Ironically the church model has in the past tended to be partial even by its own standards. The Anglican chaplain, for instance, has often ministered to liberal or high church students, developing negative relationships with evangelicals of his denomination in the Christian Union.

The third model clearly asserted the Christian perspective but in the end tended to address the university in a partial and polarized way. The 'other' was seen as the oppressor or oppressed, with the chaplain identifying with the oppressed. The outcome of this was often a failure to engage or challenge either group.

The Waterloo model is very promising in its attempts to engage the culture of the university. However, it too is very partial. It reflects a perspective from 'the platform', when in fact a university has many different cultures and layers to it. The lack of space or place even as a centre of hospitality is also a difficulty. Taking matters further than discussions in coffee bars becomes difficult, and the lack of safe space for debate or quietness limits the possibilities for engagement. The loitering with intent approach is often unfocused, and can too easily revolve entirely around the chaplain.

The final model, like the first, has the advantage of a clearly worked out role, with the chaplain as part of the student support team. The danger of this model is the loss of the autonomy of the chaplain.

With these different models there can easily be both role confusion and conflict. Chaplains are in search of a role, and institutions can be unsure how to react to someone who is connected to a major religious organization and claims entry into their midst. This is someone who they do not employ, and who they cannot control or even understand how to assess or evaluate, not least because any qualifications are not at first obviously to do with HE. At the same time if the chaplain fits too easily into the management structure of the university there is the danger of compromising the aim of mission and outreach (Moody 1999).

None of these models of themselves are able to grasp the real tension and complexity at the heart of sector ministry. There needs to be a theology that can both address how the Church can engage with this very different and complex 'other', and also retain its identity.

Theology

Moody provides a useful starting point (1999), based on the isle of Patmos. Halfway up the main hill of Patmos, between the monastery of St John and the port down below, is the cave where St John is said to have experienced the visions reported in the book of Revelation. This 'in-between' place is one of visionary experience. This is often where chaplains feel that they are located, between the Church and the institution, between the parish and the sector.

Moody offers a variety of images to give meaning to that experience. These include:

- *Wilderness ministry*. This is about the difficult experience of living without a territorial centre. In this some things are overwhelming, and there is little sense of permanence. Everything is in transition.

- *Shaman.* This is a holy figure who offers spiritual nurture and care. For many who have a sense of spiritual need, but no sense of the need for religion the chaplain is seen in this light. As such the chaplain can offer care that does attend to the human spirit, as distinct from secular counselling. She also has to deal creatively with all the expectations and projections placed on her as 'holy one'.
- *Ministry in between.* The chaplain is on the margins of both Church and university.
- *Watcher.* At one level this image might be thought of as distant. At another level it is about someone who has a valuable and valued perspective, who is not swallowed up by the institution, and who can thus see what is going on.
- *Resident Alien.* This is a popular image in many contexts (Schussler Fiorenza 1993, 335). Originally more about the care of the alien (Leviticus 19.34), the image picks up ideas of being at home and not at home at the same time, and of the chaplain being there at the invitation of the university.

Underlying Moody's images is a theology of place or position. While this is useful for illustration I believe it to be a wrong emphasis, for two reasons. First, the idea of chaplaincy as being in between runs the danger of setting up a simplistic distinction between the Church and the sector. Second, it takes away from a fundamental theology of presence, which is at the heart of incarnational theology.

Church and Sector

There is no simple view of the university or the Church as discrete, bounded or static organizations. The two different worlds are themselves complex. Neither the university nor the Church is univocal, discrete or homogeneous. The university is also in different ways a transitional community:

- By definition the individual student is in transition.
- The different student communities are transitional, sometimes lasting only a short period even within the academic year.
- Higher Education has been in transition for several decades. Change has become a way of life for staff.

The Church itself has many different narratives, in terms of theological and ecclesiological perspectives, and local context. The narratives of an inner-city parish are very different from the suburban parish and so on. Urban parishes are in communities of constant transition and change (Avis 1999). Indeed, those living in urban areas have a social identity which is minimally territorial, and territorial communities are replaced by 'pluralistic, partial communities' (Gilbert 1980). Ward takes this further, arguing that the Church has to adapt to this pluralism and build community through the 'liquid church', a series of interconnected networks (Ward 2002). The so-called solid, traditional church still has a place as refuge, but is not the first point of engagement.

On similar lines Avis argues that the simplistic division between parish (as a community primarily defined by territory) and sector no longer holds. He further argues that 'the churches' mission is seriously weakened where it is channelled exclusively through territorial structures' (Avis 1999, 13). Such territorial structures tend to stress maintenance of an exclusive group in a narrow area rather than inclusive mission.

Even the idea of operating between two areas, of Church and university, is more complex. It assumes two discrete and separate communities which are in fact interconnected in many different ways. Many Christians will teach, research or study in the university. Often there will be formal connections, such as membership on governing bodies for church leaders. Often both Church and university will share concerns about wider issues in the community. The idea of one person or even a team as standing between such institutions and somehow linking them is simplistic. However, there is a role that involves being aware of and encouraging such networks both within and between the institutions.

Incarnational Theology

Avis sees chaplaincy engagement as precisely based in incarnational theology. Chaplaincy represents Christ in and through key roles of the Church's ministry, basically worship (sacrament), pastoral care and proclaiming the gospel (Avis 1999). King adds to this the role of prophecy (King 1997). Incarnational theology, however, while it may work though these roles, is not a theology of position or place and certainly not one that stresses an intermediate position. It is rather one of presence. God was fully present as Christ. Such a presence is not distanced, but immediate, with God moving beyond himself to be one with his creation. It is just such a dynamic that Shockley sets out for chaplaincy, which he sees as the Church moving beyond itself to relate to the 'other' (Shockley 1989). This movement is also echoed in Scheler's definition of empathy. Empathy is about the person moving beyond the self and being present to the other, not simply physically there but there in the quality of attention to and concern for the other (Robinson 2001). Not surprisingly this is central to God's concern for us, and is embodied in the Trinity. Hence, Fiddes refers to God's whole being 'as empathic without reserve, as a triune event of relational love' (Fiddes 2000). Underlying this empathy is the love of God, unconditional agape that is the basis of knowing and empowering the other (Robinson 2001).

The language of empathic and loving presence, then, rather than position or place, is more suited to engagement with the other. This same language can also better accommodate the tensions expressed within Moody's list:

- *Agape* and empathy enable the person to be present to the other, to identify with him, but at the same time to have a distance (Robinson 2001). Such a distance is both epistemic and practical. If you are too close to the other you cannot truly see them or hear their developing story, nor can you practise the key caring skills (Campbell 1984). Williams writes of a detachment at the centre of such caring (Williams 1989). This is not about simply watching but about actively being with and attending to the other.
- Empathy enables the person to tell their story, reflect upon it and so hopefully to become aware of and responsible for meaning and values in that story. Clarification of underlying meaning is crucial in handling projections.
- *Agape* enables the person to be open to both sameness and difference of the other and of the self. Hence, it never allows anyone to slide into a sense of exclusive belonging on the one hand or unconnected individualism on the other.
- Empathy sets up relationships that are developing and dynamic, with the other and the self revealing their natures over time (Margulies 1989). This is not a static or 'familiar' environment but one of constant discovery, learning and creation. There is an element of constant journeying in this which is very dynamic, of never having a settled or static understanding of one environment.

This is not to dismiss the importance of the familiar. On the contrary, familiar points of reference and repose are necessary, and there are examples of both in Church and university.

All of this points to basic Johannine theology – being in the world but not of it. It points to a presence which would aim to fully belong to the different worlds of the university and the Church, understanding the culture, fears, hopes, purposes and conflicts of both, and yet be 'owned' exclusively by neither. Tawney understood this well with his stress on the need to be at home in many different environments, to be, as he put it, 'amphibious' (Tawney 1930). In all this the incarnate presence does not draw attention to itself, as the miracle at Cana shows. On the contrary such presence is often hidden, preferring to focus on the renewal of celebration and creativity. Such is also a characteristic of empathy (Robinson 2001).

This requires a genuine attention to and concern for HE and FE and at the same time a perspective that goes beyond the immediate to values and meaning that transcend this. Ultimately this locates value in the person of God, without claiming that any one group can sum up his nature and meaning.

This theology of presence, of course, is basic to all ministry not simply sector ministry, and indeed can be directly applied to the Church as a human organization. The question then is how this might be worked through in the practice of chaplaincy, how this presence might be embodied.

I suggest four heads under which a theology of presence might be considered: covenant, contract, conversation and co-creation.

Covenant

The primary relationship of the Church to HE and FE is that which embodies God's covenant. Basing this on his analysis of Old Testament writings William May (1987) outlines the covenant as:

- *Gift based*. A relationship which expects nothing in return. It embodies grace (Legood 1999).
- *Promissory*. This promises availability whatever the time or the response of the other, even if the other partner withdraws.
- *Open*. The covenant commitment defies precise specification. In

practical terms this means that the commitment cannot be predetermined, but has to be worked out in particular situations.
• *Community based*. This commitment is based in the covenant
community and relates to many different communities.

Such a covenant community embodies God's unconditional love
and active concern. Something of this is summed up in David Ford's
writing about communicating God in the university. He notes that
all communication is preceded and embraced by the communication
of God's concern and desire for each person (Ford 1999). The root
of Christ's own love is knowing that he is loved by God (1999, 7).
In the context of the university this can mean many things:

• *The development and maintenance of community*. On a modern
campus it means exploring not just traditional Christian community but also a broader sense of community, from the Internet
through to the spirituality and community of work, to effective
ecumenical community.
• *The presence of worship*. Chaplaincy can provide faithfulness in
prayer and worship throughout the year. Ford (1999) argues that
this constant rehearsal of the Christian narrative is the basis of
public communication of God on campus.
• *Unconditional care for all*. This means that the presence of
chaplaincy cannot be simply mediated through the formal structures. Chaplaincy care is there for all students and staff.
• *Prophecy*. Standing out for justice and peace is a critical part of
communicating God's word on campus.
• *Mission and outreach*. The Christian Church seeks to create
environments in which the Holy Spirit can challenge and enable
change. To be true to the covenant, chaplaincy cannot avoid this
task. But like community, mission needs sensitive, creative and
collaborative exploration, aware of the constraints of working in
an institution which is not religious.

The covenant then is the baseline for any chaplaincy. It seeks
to embody God's love, and articulate and rehearse the Christian
narrative. There may well be different Christian narratives that
emerge through that articulation, but what cannot be different is
that ultimate concern for the other. Because this covenant is one
of invitation and hospitality the narrative which is communicated

cannot be imposed, but can be faithfully rehearsed in safe contexts, ranging from debates to worship.

Such a covenant can be clearly articulated as part of any mission statement. The articulation of this is important for appointing bodies and local church groups, as well as Christians on campus, in that it provides the basis for a strategy that can include all of them. This is also important for universities, in that it assures them of the high level of provision for Christian staff and students, even purely on a consumer basis.

Contract

May distinguishes covenant from its first cousin 'contract'. Contract is specific, calculative and limits relationships. It can be put to one side if the terms of the agreement are broken. Some, such as Titmuss, have argued against the idea of contract, arguing that covenant and contract are mutually exclusive (Titmuss 1993). However, as Campbell notes in the context of healthcare they need not be (Campbell 1984). They can be used effectively together and in some cases both are necessary, provided that it is made clear how they are being used. Moreover, the idea and practice of contract has a good moral pedigree, used widely in education and pastoral care (Robinson 2001). In particular contract enables:

- Clear, mutual and realistic expectation. This includes awareness of the limitations and boundaries of any party.
- A framework for accountability.
- A framework for building up trust and value.
- A framework for establishing shared meaning.
- Mutual protection and freedom. This includes complaints procedures which demonstrate openness and transparency.

For the chaplains a contract, such as an SLA, can provide a recognized role on campus, freeing them to operate in the institution. It can reassure the institution of care offered which respects the autonomy of students and staff. Moreover, it can specify the nature of spiritual and pastoral care in a broad sense. This includes, but is much broader than, religious consumerism, enabling the institution to recognize a spiritual dimension to all care, and recognize that this can be particularly evident at moments of crisis.

Any contract, moreover, need not be static but should be revisited and refreshed on a regular basis. Such rolling contracts can then become not simply the basis for clear understanding of practice but also for reflection on the underlying values and meaning that they express. This in itself can set up fruitful dialogues, recognizing important values expressed both by the Church and also by the institution. Hence, for instance, the values of freedom of choice and tolerance, so key to the modern university campus, can be examined alongside the core values of the covenant.

Allied to this, the contract can specify how religious and spiritual pastoral care is co-ordinated, and who is responsible for this. All of this provides a way in which the academic institution can understand and value the contribution of the chaplaincy, and thus support it with appropriate resources.

The contract can make key aspects of the covenant explicit, such as unconditional pastoral care, and provides a clear *modus operandi*, within which the chaplains are accountable to the students, staff and institution. Taken together they provide the best of both worlds. The chaplaincy retains its autonomy to sing the Lord's Song, and it also belongs to that 'strange land', communicating how it relates to it and how it embodies its concern for it.

The incarnation is, of course, not based upon contract. Nonetheless, there are many points in the life of Jesus where expectations are clarified, boundaries made clear and thus forms of contract are used to enable the person to move on, be that in specific instructions to the disciples or in guidance to those who were healed.

Conversation

Ford argues that the proper style for communicating God on campus is conversational. Oakshott (1989) sees conversation as the 'peculiar virtue of a university' summed up by Ford as 'a conversation with no predetermined course, and each study not trying to dominate the others but speaking with them in a tone which is "humble and conversable"' (Ford 1999).

This sets the tone for a genuine and mutual sharing of narratives. At its base is the commitment to sustain holistic dialogue which moves across academic disciplines, worship and personal reflection, and includes affective as well as cognitive reflection. Ford suggests that this is both a preparation for the gospel and 'an expression of the Gospel appropriate to the university'. It sets up dialogic, and thus interrogative, reflection that can enable persons to take responsibility for their spirituality and hopefully discover God in that spirituality. This means that communicating the gospel is as much about listening to others and their narrative as it is about articulating our narrative of Christ. Once more it focuses on the dynamic of empathy. As Margulies (1998) notes, 'finding and creating meaning' is in itself dialectical and demands the use of empathy.

The pattern of communicating God in society tends to be either in private or through proclamation. In the first of these God is spoken of in the safe place of the 'club', where others share beliefs in club language. In the second place, communication is one-sided, centred on the God story and asking others to buy into that story. Van der Ven suggests in the context of learning values that the learning process itself is essentially intertextual, involving dialogue between the many different narratives within and outside the person (van der Ven 1998). Only that kind of conversation enables respectful clarification and challenge on cognitive and affective levels. This is equally the case for spiritual meaning and means that the communication of God in the university by definition has to be public. This may be one-to-one or between disciplines or different groups or networks. In looking at the communication and development of wisdom in universities in general Collins notes the importance of 'micro-situations', which enable face to face dialogue (Collins 1998).

The gospel, then, as Ford argues, cannot be pre-packaged but is communicated in different ways with different emphases, in and through the mutually enriching and dynamic conversation. Underlying this is the critical point that any public conversation of significance is not simply about shared interests or perspectives. That can easily fall into the club model, where different 'branches' share their view and experience. Public conversation is most effectively centred in areas of shared practice and concern, be that pastoral care, shared ethical controversies, shared concerns about education and so on. How much of the conversation will involve explicit articulation of the Christian narrative will vary, dependent upon context. The role of the chaplaincy in this is one both of enabler of and participant in these multiple conversations.

Once again we see this approach in the life of Jesus. His approach was precisely one of multiple conversations round shared problems and concerns, from one-to-one, to large groups. His use of parables was essentially narrative and conversational, always challenging the other to think about the implications of what they had said. Above all his ministry was essentially public. One can view the incarnation itself as God entering into a conversation with humanity.

Co-Creation

The presence of God in Christ made a difference to many people's view of God. Those who thought of him as judgemental and expressed in and through institutional power were presented with a loving God face to face. It led to a difference in people's lives, not least in life meaning. It led to a difference in practice and in relationships. A forgiving God enables forgiveness and reconciliation and so the development of *shalom*.

This is a theology of personal and community development, involving continual growth, creation and re-creation. Such an inclusive and dynamic vision is always greater than any one person, team, denomination or faith. Hence, the chaplaincy cannot see itself as the exclusive centre of any of the things noted above. There are many prophets struggling to find a voice on campus, Christian or not, staff or student. There are many with a concern for spiritual care. Hence, teamwork within the chaplaincy and good collaboration with others on campus and off becomes essential in enabling a creative expression of this mission.

This means recognizing and valuing areas and networks where such growth is occurring, sometimes joining networks that enable this, sometimes enabling such networks. Once again this creation and co-creation is context specific.

The creativity, which Moody sees as operating through being on the margins, is much richer in this approach. It arises from the many different perspectives that come together through dialogue. It stirs the imagination and points to possibilities, which are evermore achievable when working in collaboration with others.

Conversation and co-creation work together towards the shaping of what Carruthers (1998) refers to as *memoria*. In Ford's words this is the development of dialogic meaning which 'embraces intellect, imagination, emotion and creativity, and can be oriented to the future as to the past' (Ford 1999, 13). Importantly then the conversation is not simply about ideas, but about experience and practice and the significant meaning which emerges from reflection on these and on possibilities.

The Lord's Song

Singing the Lord's Song then is not a simple matter. It may involve many others in different ways. Intriguingly, the all-too-brief theological thoughts above would indicate that the land is not so strange after all. On the contrary it is very like the terrain in the real world, only perhaps more concentrated in certain ways. Far from plurality being strange it is in terms of this theology essential to the gospel. In one sense it would be impossible to proclaim the Word with any effect in a world where there were no other narratives with which to dialogue.

Such a plurality, as Bender (2004) notes, is itself intrinsically valuable. Without it we lose freedom and can become prey to totalitarian ways of thinking. The emphasis that the Christian faith contributes to this debate about the nature and core values of HE and FE is that plurality can only thrive if there is a secure commitment and faithfulness to maintain it (Williams 2004), if there is continually conversation between those different narratives, so that commonness as well as difference can be recognized, and if the dialogues are focused in real practice and concerns. In addition, from a Christian perspective, this provides a dialogue within which spiritual meaning can be effectively and publicly communicated and discussed.

A Christian contribution to the education debate can also be made through the stress on holistic growth and development as part of the experience of learning and education. This is a concern for many in education, not just Christians (Rogers 1983). However, once again there is a unique contribution in that the gospel takes us beyond focus on skills or capacities or even general qualities, to spiritual concerns, involving awareness and appreciation of the 'other', the capacity to respond to the other and the development of significant life meaning generated by those relationships. Along with this is a stress on the underlying development of wisdom and on learning which involves the person taking responsibility for reflection and response rather than simply the acquisition of knowledge

(Ford 1999, Hull 1991). A core part of this theology is about real learning, learning how to learn, and how learning needs someone who will accompany and challenge the learner face to face. In all this, Christian theology can affirm autonomy as a central value in education but see this as something which develops in reflective relationships, and which recognizes limitations and needs as much as desires. It stresses community and service rather than simply consumer choice and individual academic achievement (Legood 1999). It also tempers the rational-technological models of scientific thinking which as Schillebeeckx notes can distort what it is to be human (Schreiter 1986, 42)

At the heart of all this is a theology of faithfulness and truthfulness, with chaplaincy committed to being there in the midst of all the different narratives on campus. It is also a theology of hope and reconciliation.

There are many who would see HE and FE as a place of no hope, with values eroding, oppressive management practice, impossible targets being set and constant change. It would be easy for the chaplain in that light to simply man the ramparts and rail against the oncoming darkness. However, the covenant relationship is a model of hope and transformation. It believes and hopes for the best, even when things are at their bleakest as witnessed in the incarnation, death and resurrection of Jesus Christ. At the very least, hope is discovered through chaplaincy remaining faithful to all the different stakeholders throughout changes. Such faithfulness requires long-term commitment and not the short-term approach often offered by the Church in the past, with chaplains appointed for brief periods and no continuity between appointments.

Hope is also discovered and articulated in all the dialogic relationships, which provide new perspectives and all the networking, which shows how people can work together to achieve possible options. This applies both at the level of covenant, in the different groups working together for the gospel mission, and in the contract, with the many different agencies on campus collaborating. Collaborativity is one of the key elements of twenty-first century mission and care, because it enables the capacity to envisage a positive and valuable future in the midst of a present reality. In the light of this, dialogue about the core values of HE and FE will not be something for the seminar room only but an ongoing dialogue at all points of the learning and work experience.

Ultimately chaplaincy has a part to play in not just pointing to the Kingdom but also in helping to build and sustain signs of that Kingdom through the establishing of justice and peace, *shalom*, in and through the various networks. Forgiveness and reconciliation are at the heart of this, both in terms of relational dynamics and in terms of the rituals the chaplain can offer to effect or affirm these.

In one way this all points to a movement of transcendence. The development of reflectivity enables the person or group to begin to transcend the self. This enables both an awareness of the limitations of the self and others and the possibilities of the self and others. In the same way working together towards justice and peace, both within and beyond the campus, leads to a transcendence of division. Ultimately this dynamic of transcendence, always pointing beyond, can reveal something of the nature and possibilities of God himself, and how the redemption he offers can enable *shalom* (Legood 1999).

Conclusion

Who the chaplaincy represents in the light of all this will be different in different contexts. Generally the chaplain represents the Church and particularly Christ to the university. She might also represent the university in some contexts to the Church. In other pastoral contexts she might represent the university to the community, especially in context of funeral and memorial services, or the university to other universities, as in the context of student services. The representation then is not static but depends on the practices, relationships and networks that she is involved in. Far from being on the margin the chaplain will be in different positions in different contexts. Sometimes this may even be in the centre of the university community, especially in pastoral responses.

There have been many images used to suggest the role of chaplaincy in general, from jester and clown to prophet (Pattison 1994). These, however, tend to take in only limited aspects of the chaplain's role. I am arguing that the chaplaincy role, priestly, pastoral and prophetic, should be seen primarily in the context of a theology of presence and this takes into account both covenant and contract, conversation and co-creation.

Three images for me begin to sum up this. The first is of friendship. The chaplain offers in and through the different relations and networks a disciplined and attentive friendship that both affirms and challenges those involved in the light of God's love. This is the skilled companion who will accompany the different spiritual journeys being made (Campbell 1984). The second, more all embracing image, is that of accompanist. She accompanies the other in and through the different networks and dialogues. The accompanist provides a secure base without which the singer could not fully sing. At other times the accompanist will take up the song and the singer a countermelody and so on. At other times the accompanist is silent, allowing the singer to tell her own story. The aesthetic and spiritual truth of this dialogue is then a function of their co-creation, which involves both articulation and attentive listening.

A third image is that of bridge builder. As Tawney argued in the quotation at the beginning of this chapter, building bridges is a key role in modern society. The bridge allows people to cross over difficult boundaries in safety. The reality and difficulty of the boundary remains. But the bridge allows the person to enter into a different realm and return to their own, to begin to understand what is happening in that different place and to bring insights back into the home realm. In all this, chaplaincy is as much about helping people to build bridges themselves, to look beyond them and cross.

How theology such as this can be applied in practice will take up the rest of this book, looking particularly at the areas of the priestly, pastoral and prophetic.

Notes

1 I am grateful to James Bell, Diocesan Missioner of Ripon and Leeds, for this point.

References

Avis, P., 'Towards a Theology of Sector Ministry', in Legood, G. (ed.), *Chaplaincy: The Church's Sector Ministry*, Cassell, London, 1999, pp. 3–14.
Bender, T., 'Pluralism in Higher Education' in Katulushi, C. and Robinson, S. (eds), *Values in Higher Education*, University of Leeds Press, Leeds, 2004.
Campbell, A., *Moderated Love*, SPCK, London, 1984.

Campbell, A., *Paid to Care?*, SPCK, London, 1985.

Carruthers, M., *The Craft of Thought*, Cambridge University Press, Cambridge, 1998.

Collins, R., *A Sociology of Philosophies*, The Belknap Press of Harvard University Press, Cambridge, Mass., 1998.

Fiddes, P., *Participating in God*, Darton, Longman and Todd, London, 2000.

Ford, D., 'God and the University: What can we Communicate?' Paper given to the National Convention on Christian Ministry in Higher Education, High Lea, Hoddesden, 1999.

Gilbert, A., *The Making of Post-Christian Britain*, Longmans, London, 1980.

Hull, J., *What Prevents Christian Adults from Learning?* Trinity Press International, Philadelphia, 1991.

King, P., *Abnormal Ministry? Charlie Chaplaincy?* Paul King, 1997.

Legood, G., 'Universities', in Legood, G. (ed.), *Chaplaincy*, Cassell, London, 1999, 132–142.

May, W., 'Code and Covenant or Philanthropy and Contract?', in S. Lammers, and Verhey, A. (eds), *On Moral Medicine*, first edn; Eerdmans, Grand Rapids, 1987.

Margulies, A., *The Empathic Imagination*, W. W. Norton, New York, 1989.

Megone, C. and Robinson, S., *Case Studies in Business Ethics*, Routledge, London, 2000.

Moody, C., 'Spirituality and sector ministry', in Legood, G. (ed.), *Chaplaincy*, Cassell, London, 1999.

Oakshott, M., 'The Idea of a University', in Fuller, T. (ed.), *The Voice of Liberal Learning*, Yale University Press, New Haven, 1989.

Pattison, S., *Pastoral Care and Liberation Theology*, Cambridge University Press, Cambridge, 1994.

Robinson, S., *Agape, Moral Meaning and Pastoral Counselling*, Aureus, Cardiff, 2001.

Robinson, S. and Benwell, M., 'Christian Chaplaincy in a Postmodern University', *Modern Believing*, 41 (1), 2000, pp. 31–42.

Rogers, C., *Freedom to Learn*, Merrill, Columbus, 1983.

Schreiter, R. (ed.), *The Schillebeeckx Reader*, T. and T. Clark, Edinburgh, 1986.

Schussler Fiorenza, E., *Discipleship of Equals*, SCM, London, 1993.

Shockley, D., *Campus Ministry: The Church Beyond Itself*, Westminster John Knox Press, Louisville, Ky, 1989.

Tawney, R. H., *Equality*, Allen and Unwin, London, 1930.

Tawney, R. H., *Commonplace Book* (edited by J. Winter and D. Joslin), Cambridge University Press, Cambridge, 1970.

Titmuss, R., *The Gift Relationship*, Penguin, London, 1973.

van der Ven, J., *Formation of the Moral Self*, Eerdmans, Grand Rapids, 1998.

Ward, P., *Liquid Church*, Paternoster Press, Carlisle, 2002.

Williams, R., *Christianity and the Ideal of Detachment*, Clinical Theology Association, Oxford, 1989.

Williams, R., 'Faith in the University', in Katalushi, C. and Robinson, S. (eds), *Values in Higher Education*, University of Leeds Press, Leeds, 2004.

Wright, P., *Going Public*, General Synod, London, 1985.

Part 2

Priestly Work

4

Worship

When I first came to Plumpton I was determined to go to the weekly communion. By the third week I had at least three things to do in that Wednesday slot, not least the teaching that would earn me some money, and I never got back to the Chaplaincy.

I am not sure whether I miss that worship.

(Postgraduate student)

There are differing views about worship in HE chaplaincy. Some see it as central, the spine of any work that chaplains do, an embodiment of the faithful presence of the Christian community on campus. Hence, some chaplaincies put on worship every day of the week and at weekends. Others question the idea of the chaplaincy as a worshipping community, for several reasons. First, as the postgraduate above notes, it is difficult to establish a worship community in a modern university. Often there is no space for worship, no time and no commitment. Universities are very pressed and stressed places. Second, and perhaps more importantly, it is argued that the appropriate place for the worshipping community should be the local church. This provides a permanent sense of community, compared to the transient life of the student, and there are always many churches close to any university which minister to students. This parallels the approach of the Christian Union, which works on campus during the week, encouraging its members to have a 'home' church at weekends. A third argument is that the kind of rarefied atmosphere of student worship should not be encouraged. Students, it is said, who are nurtured on that always find it hard after university to get involved in the 'ordinary' church. A variation on this argument is that student worship tends to be consumerist, producing what the student wants. This does not develop the virtues of service or faith-fulness which are central to the development of a settled community.

It is certainly true that for many universities there is no space or time for the worship. Lectures go over lunch-time and even the traditional Wednesday afternoon sports time is no longer adhered to. However, the simple division between the local church and student campus worship is less clear:

- There is great diversity in student worship needs or tastes. Some are very happy to be part of many different worshipping communities, and thrive on the dialogue this creates. Others feel the need to worship in a more traditional pattern, for whatever reason. They may find themselves at different stages of their faith with different needs, some of which may be met by worship in more transitional groups.
- The idea that there is a particular thing called the local church which can be simply differentiated from rarefied student worship is not clear. In any big city there will be at least three major churches that cater for students and who, often at evening services, provide worship which is imaginative and 'rarefied'. Such services may have a very different congregation from the morning, and may be quite as consumerist as any campus student worship.

All this points to a great diversity of different worship offerings in any town, with many different needs expressed by the student. In one sense then all the chaplaincy needs to do is to bring the students to the great range of churches and all will be catered for. This is an important function of chaplaincy, partly fulfilled by the production of a local churches directory. All local churches can be contacted, and those who want to be in the directory contribute a self-description and contact details. However, while it is important to embrace diversity this does not help us with the question of what the argument for campus worship might be.

In this chapter I will examine this, consider the worship needs in different areas on and off campus, and finally focus on one example of pastoral worship which illustrates how worship on campus can involve all aspects of ministry.

Why Worship

Avis (1999) suggests that two of the key elements of ministry in chaplaincy are the word and sacrament. At one level this is for the benefit of Christians on campus, reinforcing their faith. It is also a witness to those who are not part of the Church, to the communities that make up the university. Ford (1999, 8) takes this further to argue that worship is the linchpin of any public communication of God on campus. Ford is clear that it does not really matter how many attend. It is the fact that worship is available and that the rehearsal of the God story is there on campus which is important. Such worship does several things:

- It links to the historical narrative of the wider Church, resonating 'with generations of communication with God'.
- It enables communities and groups to enter into that story. Thus while there is the rehearsal of a historical narrative the intensive experience of worship also creates new meaning. As Ford puts it, the meaning is 'improvised upon through non-identical repetition'.
- It 'informs and forms' communities and their members in various ways. This is partly about providing the distinctive view of the gospel and partly about developing the virtues of the Christian community, not least wisdom and the desire for wisdom. Such worship is then holistic, engaging meaning at cognitive, affective, somatic and social levels.
- It shapes the overall conversation, referred to in Chapter 4, about God. This is both within the Church, between members of the same traditions and between different traditions, and in the broader university community.

This intensity of focus with others on God provides the basis of what Ford calls a healthy ecology of Christian communication on campus. It is not the exclusive way to communicate. The pastoral, prophetic and teaching approaches all enable the kind of conversation that Ford extols. But if there is no worship within the university, articulating the Christian story in all its diversity, then the other aspects of conversation, the public communication of God, and the enabling of conversation lose the critical reference point.

Having set out the essential part that worship plays in communicating God on campus, Ford then makes it clear that how this is to be achieved on campus is a problem not for him as theologian, but for the chaplain!

The practical answer is perhaps found in the linking of community and worship. Much like Hauerwas (1998, 11) he sees worship at the centre of community. However, Hauerwas has a very fixed and bounded view of community. The reality for university work is that there is no such fixed community. Instead there are many different kinds of community, each of which can be involved in some way in the public communication of God. Developing worship on campus then is not a function of finding different forms of worshipping, modern or academic, but rather in finding and affirming or developing the many different communities, and encouraging the worship which informs their different natures, and affirms their common root in Christ.

Worshipping Communities

The different worshipping areas on campus include:

- Chaplaincy worship.
- Christian student groups on campus.
- The university community and institutional rites.
- The interface between university, chaplaincy and city.
- Rites of passage.
- Pastoral crises.

Chaplaincy Worship

It is clear from all these that the chaplaincy is not the only Christian group on campus, and that it cannot claim in any sense to be 'over' the other groups. However, many of the other groups are transitional, meeting only during semester or parts of semesters. At the same time, the university itself is a year-round community and worship from the chaplaincy can provide a year round presence.

That presence embodies faithfulness to the wider community and to the historical community of the Church and to the God story. It should also embody a sense of inclusiveness. How such worship is developed will depend upon the local context. One chaplaincy focused on a 'family meal' on Wednesday evenings. Funds were provided for students on a rota to make the meal. Around the meal a series of rituals grew up, welcoming everyone, presenting a menu and so on. After the meal a worship service developed. The service was intentionally only half an hour long, giving people the chance to get back to work or go out. It had a basic framework with students creating parts of it each week. The community which built up was not a discrete and bounded chaplaincy community. It was made up of students from different Christian groups and those with no affiliation, a community of communities. This tradition has been maintained for over 20 years, with numbers ranging from 20 to 100.

Another chaplaincy had a campus communion every Wednesday lunch-time. Like the previous example this was intentionally ecumenical, pointing to a community which was non-exclusive. For this team, holy communion embodied the essential gospel narrative and acted as the basis of reflection. The communions of different traditions were used on a rota basis, something that the students and staff valued. The service itself was tailored to fit into 25 minutes, with 30 minutes for a bread and cheese lunch afterwards. Hence, it was seeking to fit into the community of which it was a part. There may be no single 'community' that fits into this worship, rather involving different communities in and out of term.

Another chaplaincy focused on Sunday evenings as the key time for worship. While this did not operate at the centre of the working community it was in an area where the majority of students lived reasonably close to the campus or at home. This formed a community which thrived around non-eucharistic reflective worship, including Taizé worship, and then moved on to food and discussion afterwards.

The ecclesiology of the different members of any chaplaincy team may not feel fully at home with these kinds of ecumenical worship. Commonly the Roman Catholic chaplain and some Anglicans will want to maintain worship in their specific tradition. Again there is no problem with this diversity, provided it is seen to be part of the overall chaplaincy presence. One chaplaincy team has worship provided by Quakers, Roman Catholics, Greek Orthodox, Anglican, and Chinese Christian Church. All are aware of and articulate their relationship to wider chaplaincy. Perhaps equally importantly the rest of the community is able to see the many different worship events occurring in the same building or buildings at different times or together. Hence, it is able to get some sense of a community of communities, with worship enabling awareness of both sameness and difference.

Many things can support this central worship life, including:

- Developing a prayer list that goes out to every Christian, student or staff, noting both the time and place of different acts of worship and people on campus who are being prayed for that month. This way even if a person cannot make it to worship they can join in prayer for five minutes, and feel a part of the wider worshipping community on campus.
- The chaplaincy, in collaboration with different student and staff groups, can begin to develop worship which brings together the different Christian groups on campus. This is not simply about shared ecumenical worship, involving the 'denominations', but can include the many different student groups which have no home in any denomination, such as SCM or Christian Medical Fellowship. Such worship affirms and strengthens networks, sets up the chance for real intertextual dialogue, and recognizes that there are things and times of importance, which transcend any particular groups or concern for group issues. To facilitate this it is important to develop a season of worship that brings together different groups in a natural way so that this is not just a question of finding an excuse to meet. There is a view that the university is not well suited to regular worship. The majority of students are not there for the two major festivals of the year, and not there for the whole of the summer. However, while the university does not fit easily into the Church's year it does have its own points of reflection. These provide the basis of many different services, including:

Semester 1

- Intro-week welcome service. This could be simply a variation of the weekday service, or could be one that brings together representatives from the local churches so that they can meet students after the service. Many local churches find this an important opportunity.
- Major ecumenical service. This could be worked around the occasion of One World Week. Such a service can link not

simply into the Christian networks but also the wider networks such as the international student office, the equality office and the different international student groups.

- Major community/university service such as a university sermon.
- A major retreat or weekend away, open to any students.
- Advent service. This can be quite a formal occasion.
- Carol service. The importance of the carol service cannot be underestimated. Any chapel choir can provide the basis for this. Even more interesting is where the chaplaincy has to bring together groups from throughout the university – various student orchestras and choirs.

Semester 2

- Lent worship.
- Christian Aid Service – connected to all the different Christian groups collecting money in the different halls of residence.
- Services can be worked around events such as Christian Awareness Week.
- Farewell Service. Chaplaincies produce many different approaches to this. One chaplaincy, for instance, produced an early morning communion on the moors, before going on to breakfast and a day's activity.

Sacred Space

If worship is a central part of what King (1997) calls the 'come' ministry, inviting all *to* the chaplaincy, then there has to be proper space for it. Again this will vary from campus to campus. Some will have a chapel that is central. Some will have split sites, where there is no obvious centre. Each team has to focus on the most appropriate centre of their worship life. One team had three different operational sites, each of which provided worship at some point tailored to the communities in question. Whatever the arrangement, there has to be that sense of the sacred space as being inviting and as being a home for all the different Christian groups and more.

Different Christian Student Groups

Alongside chaplaincy there are different autonomous groups including

- *Student worship groups* such as CU, SCM, Christian Medical Fellowship and the Catholic Society. For the most part these groups organize their own worship. Sometimes a chaplain is central to that – as in Roman Catholic Mass. Sometimes the chaplain is only one of many involved in organizing worship, sometimes there is no involvement at all. Such student groups are largely not formed on denominational lines, and their worship can range from what used to be called experimental to alternative, such as Taizé worship. Each group has its own context and purpose. Where any student group is largely marginal (Jamieson 2002, 158) a chaplain can link with them and encourage worship that is both reflective and student focused, and also connective, i.e. linking in to the wider Church through content and style. Hence, the group can still be in a position to explore its relationship to that wider Church and not cut itself off.
- *Halls of residence worship groups.* Some halls of residence have some form of worship, including student cell groups and even some local church presence.
- *Departmental prayer groups.* On the increase, such groups often meet weekly, and sometimes attempt to include staff. Again it is useful for a chaplain to touch base with such groups, embodying a sense of Christian solidarity in their worship.
- *Interest groups.* There may be different groups on campus, for instance in performing arts or music, who have developed worship in various ways, often in the grey area between performance and worship. One department of music, for instance, developed a liturgical choir. This put on various services as part of the MA in liturgy and music. Such worship can be networked in many different ways, inviting the Christian community as a whole, with such groups taking key roles in Christian and broader community worship.

While the chaplain cannot 'claim' any of these groups, things do vary from place to place. In a university with little space or time it might be that the chaplain will collaborate closely with the Christian

Union, in some cases the only Christian group on campus, to produce significant services, such as the carol service. One FE chaplain intentionally formed a CU in his college.

So what we have developing are networks of worship in which different transitional groups collaborate. The whole has a feel of many different pilgrims, on different but related journeys which chaplains or related groups such as local churches can affirm and help to grow in relation to national and local groups. Because the chaplaincy is central it is the best place to provide the underpinning of the supportive worship of many of these groups in different contexts. It is not the job of chaplaincy to have all this under its wing, but to enable the different groups to relate through worship.

University Worship

The university itself has its own seasons, with times of importance which can be marked in ritual and which provide an opportunity for worship mediated dialogue. In some respects this reflects the life cycle of the student (see Chapter 7), and at other points it intersects with the Christian seasons. Here are just a few possibilities that have a strong institutional feel to them:

- *Celebratory worship*, such as the intro-week welcome and the carol service. These can be as much a celebration of the wider community as of the Christian network. The carol service can come in all shapes and sizes from the traditional nine lessons and carols based on the musical talent of the institution to dramatic events. One FE chaplain produced a carol service on the theme of the X-Files, entitled the Xmas-Files.
- *Transitional worship*, such as graduation services. While such services are traditionally a celebration of the students' success, they can also be a ritual focus, reflecting on the time of transition.

  The graduation season is a good example of how difficult it can be to fit services in. Some universities with large halls might have only two or three graduations ceremonies. With so many people together around a ceremony then it is possible to plan for a large service. Even then it will have to be at a time that fits easily into the timetable of photographs, fittings and food. Other universities have as many as thirty ceremonies over two weeks, making the programme and focus even more hectic and fragmented. Nonetheless, it is possible to provide much more intimate services for much smaller groups. One example of this is where only two people turned up. Somewhat disgruntled, the chaplain did the service and then engaged mother and daughter in conversation. To his surprise the daughter said that this had been the most important part of her day. Her father had died in the second semester of her last year and she had been given help by another chaplain. She commented, 'It was so right for me to touch base with the chaplaincy and more important to include my dad in today's events.' This is also a good example of how purposive presence can engage with great depth in a very short period of time.

- *Significant departmental events.* A good example is the biomedical sciences memorial service held annually to give thanks for those who donated their bodies to the school. This is an important point of reflection for the students and staff. It is also a crucial moment for the families. For many there is a sense that only after such a service could they feel at peace. It is possible to involve students in all aspects of such a service, including its co-creation. Co-creating such a service forces the students and chaplain to be aware of the families, most of whom want a Christian service, and of the students, many of whom have little understanding of Christian concepts. One student began his reflection with the words, 'working with the bodies in biomedical science has taught me more about what it is to be human than anything else the course this year'. He then went on describe respect for the person in all his or her limitations and creative possibilities. It is also possible to develop rituals that have immediate effect on all the different groups in the service. The central act of remembrance, for instance, is often one of everyone filing up to light candles on the altar while music is being played and the names of the donors are read out. After the service, students, families and staff intermingle and continue the three-way dialogue.
- *Major one-off events*, such as centenary celebrations or responses to times of crisis, such as September 11th. These provide a good opportunity for multifaith reflection on education and its values. This would not be genuine multifaith worship but would be more sharing of prayers and perspectives. Such events bring together many different parts of the university at times of crisis.

- *Annual community events.* A good example of this is Remembrance Day. One chaplaincy holds a brief but very significant service on 11 November. The chapel is always filled. This can focus on the students lost in conflict, and brings together academic staff, support staff and students.

Church Links

There are many ways of linking into local churches through worship, including:

- Intro-week services at the university that include local church representatives, as noted above.
- Once or twice a semester to have university sermons which bring major figures and which are open to the public. This can allow all the local churches to take advantage of what a university ought to do well.
- Focusing on 'Education Sunday' for events in the local churches where choirs and groups can work together. This could take the form of a 'civic' service.
- Chaplains and students going out to local churches, devising services and affirming links.
- The number of international students in HE and FE provides opportunities to link into the worldwide Church in very tangible ways, with students contributing to local church services and enabling links.

Such links enable worship with a wide intertextual dialogue, connecting university groups to local need and vice versa.

Rites of Passage

Tom Scott, a great Scottish chaplain, established chaplaincy at Heriot Watt, Edinburgh. The university there eventually moved out to a purpose-built campus on the edge of the city. The chaplaincy centre provided a 'home from home'. Two students were resident, and there were meeting rooms and a very flexible worship area. In a ministry of 13 years Tom conducted 115 weddings and 28 baptisms.

For some there are major issues here. Should the chaplain get involved in such events? Is it not more appropriate that the local church take on certain rituals, especially baptism? It is not the role of this book to resolve such debates. It is worth, however, drawing attention to the fact that even transitional communities and their members also need rites of passage to begin to develop spiritual meaning at critical moments of change.

Mary, for example, was an international MA student. She gave birth to her first child some seven months into a twelve-month course. She was supported in her pregnancy by fellow students, chaplaincy and members of the international student club. She needed many things from the baptism of her baby:

• Public recognition and affirmation of her child and herself as a one-parent family.
• Affirmation of her transitional community.
• Confirmation of this as part of the worldwide Church.

Preparation for the service was done first with a one-to-one discussion which allowed her to articulate all these needs through talking about her story. Then over a further two sessions she and one of the chaplains began to construct the baptism in the light of these considerations. The service took place as part of the regular worship on campus and was followed by food and celebration that linked back to her own country.

For Mary the experience of great change in a strange land took on very real meaning. She eventually became a regular at one of the chaplaincy Sunday services.

Styles of Worship

From all this it is clear that there is no single style of worship that can be designated as 'student worship'. Indeed many students want conventional worship. It is, however, important to be abreast of the latest music and styles from events such as Spring Harvest and Greenbelt. However, the experts in that are the students themselves, and thus the key to development of chaplaincy worship is to focus on the communities and enable the students involved to take responsibility for worship in the light of their needs and learning. As

Baker, Gay and Brown (2003) note, 'alternative worship' is not 'youth ministry' but rather involves the development of worship in the context of a particular community. This involves the development of rituals and resources that are appropriate and stimulating. One example of such a resource is the use of the labyrinth (www. labyrinth.org.uk). Based on the labyrinth floor pattern of Chartres Cathedral this enables a walking meditation, moving into the centre and then out. With candles and music it provides a powerful reflective and relaxing tool. It can also be used in a wider community context for staff as well as students.

In their book *Alternative Worship* (2003) Baker, Gay and Brown include an invaluable list of resources, and guidance on how tradition in worship can be valued and also reframed.

The chaplain should be alive to the different possibilities and to ways in which these may be used or brought together. One example of this is the development of a campus-wide mission, where tradition and alternative worship can be creatively coordinated.

Pastoral Care and Worship

It is clear from what I have written so far that worship on campus cannot be contained in a small box marked 'worship'. On the contrary worship which is reflective and dialogic will be moving into all the other areas of ministry. Events around Education Sunday or the university sermon, for instance, will provide a space for prophetic proclamation about the values in Higher Education, and this in turn will reinforce pastoral work which is dealing with the effects of perfectionism and conditional life-scripts on students and staff. Worship in small groups, or in response to departmental needs, can provide the ritual reflection at the centre of a genuinely learning organization.

Pastoral care and worship come together most strikingly in the care of bereaved students and family after a student death. There is little understanding of mourning for the modern student and how this might relate to grief. Mourning is precisely a public and often ritual response to bereavement, a way of expressing grief which involves shared practice and, with that, finding shared meaning of some kind. For the majority of students there is neither. Hence, for many there are two key questions or observations when experiencing bereavement: 'How should I feel? I don't know what to feel', and 'What should I do?'

The funeral is one way in which these questions can be focused. However, many funerals assume a shared religious background and thus may exclude a majority of students present. The exploration of spiritual meaning, in its broadest sense, is something which takes place well after the funeral, as the students or family members reflect on what has happened.

Connecting all these different explorations, and thus helping the student to connect grief and mourning, can be achieved through the development of an appropriate memorial service (Robinson 2002). Such services help the family to 'locate' the deceased, and know more of the life they did not share. For the student they form a shared ritual in which meaning can be explored.

Some memorial services, particularly if the deceased is an international student, are requested within 48 hours of the death. This then gives the parents an immediate feel for the distant community that their child was a part of, and the value of their child in and to that community. For parents this can provide a way to focus any spiritual meaning, which will inform the later funeral. More often the service will be a month or two after the funeral. At the other extreme was one service that was a year and three months after the death of the student: the only time when all the cohort could come together again was when they graduated, over a year later.

Co-creating the Service

The creation of the service brings together all the major parties in some way. In many cases this means that students will involve representatives of several different groups. One student who was killed in a traumatic accident was a member of five different groups. Representatives of all the groups came together with members of the family and a chaplain. With the aim of developing an order of service the group met for five sessions, and three interconnected functions were fulfilled, pastoral, spiritual and liturgical:

1 Each group shared something of their narrative about the deceased and her significance to that group. These became the core of the service. With sharing of stories there also emerged pastoral problems that were part of the grief. In the case of the society which

was involved in the accident, the members told the story in some detail. This was important for all the other groups to hear, as part of their grieving process. They encouraged that sharing in a non-judgemental way, helping the society to deal with any guilt. All the while trust was growing between the different groups such that they were able to challenge each other in a non-aggressive way. The society, for instance, did not want to mention the incident on its website, for fear that it would put off future students from joining. The memorial service group was able to help them reflect on this so that they were not denying this incident as a part of their club life. The role of the chaplain in all this was to enable the stories to be told and enable the different groups to listen to each other, and thus develop empathy and mutual support.

2 Values and life meaning emerged from the stories told by the groups about the person. These partly reflected her personal values and partly the values of the groups. The task of the chaplain here was to help the different groups to draw out the underlying meaning. The different values that emerged could then be reflected on. Some-times this involved reflection on values that seemed contradictory. These may be values of the person, such as a strong sense of care and responsibility for others but not for herself, or values shared by the different groups. Once again the task of the chaplain was not to judge between values but rather to enable the larger group to be aware of the different values and take responsibility for handling them.

Christian values emerged as part of that whole dialogue. The deceased, in this case, was a Christian and thus such values naturally became part of the reflection. In other situations the family members may have some religious faith which becomes part of the reflection. On some occasions members of the group might ask the chaplain about her faith, and how it relates to the event. This may also come up as a negative view of traditional funeral services. In all this the Christian spirituality becomes a part of any reflection on the life and community of the deceased but is not the driving force or the primary way of viewing her. This also means that any Christian spirituality is actually tested through the dialogue, its sameness and difference from other world-views being clarified.

3 On a more formal level, values and spirituality emerge from the consideration of secular and religious readings, songs and rituals for the event itself. Each group is able to recognize the different

meanings, test them out and so own them as part of the reflective process and the event itself. In this case it led to reflection on the idea and purpose of prayer, and how it could be enabled in the service in such a way that all could feel involved. For many non-Christians prayer was seen as 'reaching out beyond' or 'tapping into transcendence'. The solution for the service was the use of candles as a focus of prayer, allowing all to come to the front to light them as part of the service. Such rituals can tap into meaning at cognitive, affective and somatic levels. The somatic side is often addressed by photographs – perhaps at the entrance, so that people can focus on physical memories before and after the service. Increasingly, multimedia resources are used, combining music, computer images, and projected photographs and texts. All of this increases the number of people who are involved in the creation of the service.

It is worth also mentioning the site for the service. Once again the group decides this, and once again it is a decision which reflects something about meaning, be it an open-air service, or one in the student union main hall, or one in the chapel. Moreover, depending on where the service is sited this enables even more people to be involved in helping with its realization. It also enables different sites to be seen as having special and even sacred use.

The memorial service as outlined above can provide a framework within which the different groups and individuals can safely dialogue about the spiritual meaning of their loss, and establish rituals for sharing that meaning. The presence of the chaplain is a key to enabling this reflection. Without claiming a privileged status for the Christian narrative the chaplain can sum up the very different values involved.

Conclusion

The chaplain and chaplaincy team then take on a priestly role in relation to the chaplaincy community, to the broader Christian community and the wider institution community and communities. This involves a range of worship provision from the traditional sacramental approach to alternative worship, to worship which develops meaning in response to pastoral crises. All of this sets up the conversation and *memoria* which Ford sees as central to worship on campus, and issues of particular worship traditions are secondary to this.

However, there is, as Tawney noted, another sense of priesthood, which focuses on building bridges in a much broader way.

References

Avis, P., 'Towards a Theology of Sector Ministry', in Legood, G. (ed.), *Chaplaincy*, Cassell, London, 1999.

Baker, J., Gay, D., and Brown, J., *Alternative Worship*, SPCK, London, 2003.

Ford, D., 'God and the University: What can we Communicate?' Paper given at National Convention on Christian Ministry in Higher Education, High Lea, Hoddesden, 1999.

Hauerwas, S., *Sanctify Them in the Truth*, T. and T. Clark, Edinburgh, 1998.

Jamieson, A., *A Churchless Faith*, SPCK, London, 2002.

King, P., *Abnormal Ministry? Charlie Chaplaincy?*, Paul King, Edinburgh, 1997.

Robinson, S., 'Thanks for the memory . . . Death of a student: Memorials, mourning and postmodernity', *Contact* 138, 2002, pp. 16–25.

5

Building Bridges

It has taken new student John and his family four and half hours to get to Plumpton and now the real problems begin. He is in a hall of residence in a suburb of Plumpton and it takes him a further two hours to get there. Once he arrives he is shown to his room by a returning student, who makes him feel at home, but thereafter communication overload takes over and does not stop for a week.

On Sunday the hall wants him to be clear about the rules and regulations and just what a good deal he can get on the vodka promotional evenings on Wednesday, Thursday and Friday. On Monday John makes it to the department and is taken for a guided tour around the campus, and then back for several different talks from the staff about the department. Then he goes off to the union for their welcome party. Tuesday, he's back in the union for their orientation programme, and another tour around campus, stopping for long periods at the library, the union building, and the student medical practice. That night is the departmental welcome party, which features a good deal of vodka. Wednesday sees John heading for registration where he is bombarded with massive numbers of leaflets. Being polite, he does not want to throw them on the floor like most others. Registration involves long queues and waits for ID cards, and leads into the electives fair. This has stalls for departments and different agencies that provide elective modules. The evening sees more vodka at the departmental student society inaugural 'bash'. By Thursday John is ready to face the societies' bazaar. This is a chance to decide which of the societies he might like to join. He chooses four interesting societies, all of which have intro events that evening and Friday evening. All of which involve vodka. By Saturday John is disorientated and homesick. The reality of Monday and lectures comes as something of a welcome.

John's intro-week is only average. Some have more lonely ones. Others reach much greater hedonistic heights. How is the chaplaincy to reach him? Should they indeed try to do so, or should they feel that likely students will come to them whatever?

Waiting is in one sense no option. First, the university is on the whole too big for the chaplaincy to be seen easily from the beginning. Second, the chaplaincy is not there for the faithful alone. They can be reached through various routes. The chaplaincy needs to get across its presence in different ways, such that its mission can be maximized. This is not about creating an image but rather about communicating the different ways in which chaplaincy and the wider Church is present for the student and staff. As Tawney reminded us in Chapter 4, this making of connections is another dynamic view of what it is to be a priest. It can be summed up in the idea of networking. Networking is often seen as something which is additional to the ministry. You do the ministry and then you network. Networking, however, is fundamental to sector ministry. It can be defined as building up purposive relationships which can enable the widest and most creative mission and outreach. The idea of relationships built around purpose, and thus practice, is central to this approach. The average student union key worker, central administration or academic staff member does not have the time, or for that matter the inclination, simply to get to know the chaplain. If it is not followed up in meeting and action, the lunch at the beginning of term/semester will be forgotten by the third week, 'That chaplain showed an interest but I'm not sure why we met or what he does.' Significant relationships are built up around shared concerns, collaboration and practice that make a difference.

There are three major kinds of networking:

- Mutual, in which the two parties help each other in different aims.
- Communal, where the parties work together for the same aim.
- Instrumental, where one of the parties involved acts on behalf of the other(s).

Such networking can be employed to reach students in many

different ways during intro-week. A checklist of such networking might include the following:

Intro-week Networking

- Two months before the intro-week information about chaplaincy is given out to the student office to be sent out to new under graduates. This may involve a tear-off slip, for follow-up enquiries.
- A meeting with local church leaders before the start of term helps to ensure good working together in intro-week.
- One to two weeks before the event the chaplains may send out letters to those who have responded to invite them to events in intro-week.
- Chaplains who have links into the halls of residence may be at the hall when the students arrive, and involved in the welcome.
- Chaplains who have strong links to the student support services may be involved in introducing the student support services as a whole to new students in halls.
- Chaplaincy may work closely with local churches in a welcome service for new students so that they can meet with local church representatives after the service.
- Close work with the Christian Union. One CU has had a 'Big Tent' which the chaplaincy was able to find a prime site for. A chaplain might be frequently around the Tent with publicity for chaplaincy and for the local churches. This might include leaflets for the student elective modules offered by the chaplaincy (see Chapter 10).
- The chaplains might be present at their welcome evenings of other student groups, such as SCM.
- Close work with strongly evangelistic churches might lead to the provision of food at an open air café during the week.
- The chaplaincy team might oversee a number of welcome parties at the different sites.
- A chaplain might be present at registration, supporting staff and being available to students.

- Information about the chaplaincy may be received through the student handbook, and the student support services handouts. The latter, be they wall planners, credit-card size handouts or bookmarks, set chaplaincy in the context of student support and care.
- The chaplain may receive an invitation via the student services network to attend welcomes put on for international students, postgraduates, etc.

This is not an exhaustive list but simply a flavour of how the chaplaincy can be present in and through a wide variety of networks in the intro-week. At all the crucial points of the experience, in hall, in department, in registration or at receptions, the chaplaincy is given the chance to be there. In other events through networks the chaplaincy is able to be a part of a wider Christian outreach. This would be true for the individual chaplain or for the team. However, with different members of the team being part of different networks the presence is maximized.

Developing effective networks takes time. It can involve three broad approaches:

- Joining already established networks – such as the student services.
- Setting up new networks, e.g. for global ethics.
- Taking part in maintaining networks.

These can be seen in terms of covenant and contract. Covenant networks seek to maximize the church presence on and off campus demonstrating that the Christian presence is much greater than the chaplaincy. Contract networks involve work with other university agencies. Some networks pick up both elements.

The setting up and maintaining of networks demands attention to meeting cycles, protocols and maintaining rhythm. For instance, an interfaith student network needs to meet soon after the student religious societies' cycle of annual meetings to link into the new committees and maintain communication.

Christian Networking on Campus

It is always hard to estimate the number of Christians on any campus. Some want to be associated with Chaplaincy, others wish to remain anonymous. Others may see a chance to contribute to Christian outreach via discrete events.

The Christian Union

It is important to begin with the CU because this is generally the biggest Christian student group on campus.

In the 1960s and 1970s there was a strong sense of the Christian Union being in conflict with chaplaincy in many universities. As in all such conflicts there was a strong element of mutual stereotyping.

The CU was seen as doctrinally conservative, biblically literal, having no sense of the political or social dimension of the gospel, and with little sense of differences within the group. All in all they were perceived by many in the Student Christian Movement (SCM) – which was often associated with the chaplaincy – as having cultic tendencies, which above all would stop free thinking. Hence, when chaplains met together the first items on the agenda were always the CU 'horror stories'. This often led to chaplaincies identifying themselves negatively, as not like the CU. The CU often saw itself as the bastion of orthodoxy and right theology. To this day it has a declaration of faith which all members must sign when they join.

In contrast the CU saw the chaplaincy as a place which was liberal, on the whole not biblical, and which could put students off the right path. The SCM was also frowned upon, referred to as the 'Slightly Christian Movement'.

In fact, modern CUs are very different. We are in a post-evangelical age, with greater concern about mission through the development of friendship. There are many different kinds of Christian within the CU, as noted above, such that there is a great deal of openness and reflection. Modern CUs are often aware of the complexity and ambiguity of many issues, and are very open to collaboration. This can include:

- Working together to monitor and respond to cults or new religious movements.
- Carol services. The CU often produces very popular carol

concerts in contrast to formal university carol services. It is possible to work together on both. In smaller institutions this might involve collaboration in one service.

- Christian Aid Week. CU cell groups can collect envelopes, giving them more entry into different areas.
- Intro-week. As noted above chaplaincy can provide resources, and the CU network is a way of mediating chaplaincy presence.
- In the halls, through midweek services, and through cell groups.

It is important then for the chaplaincy to be in touch with the CU and in particular to ensure that one member of the team is a link person. Ideally, he or she should be on the CU honorary advisors group. In turn the chaplaincy can link in with the CU through their curriculum provisions, as outlined in Chapter 10.

Other Christian Student Groups

There might be many other Christian societies on campus. Like the CU these are autonomous student union societies, which are accountable to the student union. It is important to have chaplains linking into these groups in enabling and resourcing roles, without affecting their autonomy.

Christian Liaison

The chaplain can also enable Christian groups to network among themselves through the development of a Christian network or liaison group. The aim of such a group is to find ways of sharing news and ideas, and to work together in mission where appropriate. A good example of this is the development of a Christian Awareness Week. This can involve the groups putting on different events and providing displays and stands in central places in the university and union. In effect it is a mini-mission.

Christian Staff

Chaplaincy can enable Christian staff to meet together and discuss common issues, or even to organize events for the university or for their department or faculty.

Interfaith Networking

There is now pressure from many universities for chaplaincies to network effectively with other faiths. Some modern universities are keen to organize interfaith chaplaincies. The impetus behind this is basically to do with religious rights – that the university should ensure that all religions are catered for, with no faith taking a privileged position. This is an important aim, and any chaplaincy service should embrace this. There are, however, problems.

- Often there is no recognized local or national faith body which can actually appoint one of its leaders to the role of chaplain. Attempts have been made in the Muslim tradition to form such a body. However, they do not have the finances to pay for chaplains or advisors and the responsibility for appointing them comes down to the local Muslim organization. For the most part, however, there is no Muslim local 'ecumenical' group that would or could appoint such a person.
- Where there is a national body that could appoint, as in the case of Orthodox Jews (the National Jewish Chaplaincy Board), this tends to lead to appointments which cover a large number of universities.
- The vast majority of leaders of other faiths are concerned first and foremost about the nurture and pastoral care of their own flock. There is usually nothing in their brief about co-ordinating the work of other faiths or about a broader view of pastoral care – offered to any student – or about a more student-centred view of pastoral care and counselling.

All of this means that it is not possible to have a chaplaincy in which other faiths play an inclusive or organizational role. It might of course be possible if the university were to appoint a non-denominational chaplain. For the most part, however, it is only a non-denominational or specifically Christian ecumenical model which accepts a wider, more inclusive approach.

The chaplaincy team and co-ordinator then have a dual role, to coordinate inclusive spiritual and pastoral care, and to co-ordinate care and support for students of particular religions, which will involve effective networking with all faiths. Such a network might include:

- Regular conversation with the different representatives of other faiths on campus.
- Establishing links to a national interfaith network (Gilliat-Ray 2000, 177).
- Establishing an interfaith network or liaison group on campus.

In establishing any such groups two things are important:

1 The remit of the groups should be as exact as possible. Though Boyce (2002) argues that there are sound Christian reasons for working with other faiths, such as the inclusive nature of the incarnation, many Christian groups are wary of 'selling out' to other faiths, especially in the area of joint worship. Hence, it is important to be clear about the function of the group, and that this does not include multifaith worship. The functions might include:

- Working together to explore each other's faith, thereby encouraging awareness of and respect for the different faiths.
- Setting up events to help others explore the different faiths. A good example of this is the organization of a Faith Awareness Week, involving debate, dialogue and displays throughout the campus.
- Responding to times of crisis. A good example of this was September 11th. For many this involved both response to the tragedy itself and to subsequent ill-feeling about faith groups, both Jewish and Muslim. This included many public debates which aimed to model respect and care.

2 The members of the network should be carefully chosen. Ideally the network should include representatives from the university administration, the student union, different faith groups and chaplains. With this all the major groups will feel that they own this area and own any statement or charter of religion that they might want to develop for the institution (Gilliat-Ray 2000, 179). Such a group can be the place where issues of student religious rights are explored and communicated to the university.

Universities, on the whole, have responded well to some of the basic issues of interfaith needs, such as provision for religious festivals that clash with exams. However, interfaith liaison groups can ensure that religion is a significant part of the university and one, moreover, in certain contexts, which can lead to some real contributions to the community. Such groups can keep the university aware of the European directives on religious equality.

In addition to such meetings it may be important for the different chaplains and religious leaders to meet at least once a term to monitor faith and pastoral relationships.

Christian Networking Off Campus

There are many different networks that can be developed with Christian groups off campus, including:

- Guiding the students to the different churches. The production of a churches handbook for students (also kept on the chaplaincy website) can help with this.
- Chaplains can regularly visit local churches with a good student population.
- Inclusion of local clergy as part of the team, through enabling pastoral care opportunities in halls of residence that may be in their parish.
- Some denominations may choose to network via local organizations, such as deaneries.
- Working with local church buildings, making them available for student groups.
- Linking in student groups to the local church, e.g. through leading occasional worship.
- Linking in to local church volunteers, e.g. for weekday cafés, international student clubs, or intro-week.
- Developing forums for debate, especially about subjects that are controversial in the local churches. In this the campus can provide a safe space for such discussions.
- Developing collaborative mission events.

All such links can significantly affect mission and mediate presence, while also improving the best student experience.

Networking in the Institution

Networking in the institution both uses the usual systems of committee and management, and also goes beyond this, demonstrating the breadth of concern for Higher and Further Education.

Management

The concerns of chaplaincy for management should be inlcusive. It is important therefore to:

- Work at setting up a relationship with the vice-chancellor. This is both an expression of pastoral care and also an opportunity to reflect on the way in which the institution is going. Most vice-chancellors see this as an opportunity for sharing 'intelligence' – finding a perspective on the shop floor which would not be filtered by partial interest.
- Link in with the university secretary and the different pro-vice-chancellors, especially those for staff and students.
- Make contact with the equal opportunities office. This would involve concern for religious rights, cultural and ethical interests.
- Become involved in university committees, and where necessary help to set these up. These might include:

  - Ethics committees, for research or medicine.
  - Student support committees. The chaplaincy will need to chart the different committee structure of each university, including related committees on mental health, drugs and alcohol. One of the burgeoning areas of concern in mental health recently has been spirituality (Robinson, Kendrick and Brown 2003). The chaplain can contribute reflection on this, looking at issues of hope, purpose and faith in relation to mental health. In this area the chaplain can help to take the perspective beyond the liberal and utilitarian approaches.
  - Senate, court or council. There may be ways of becoming part of one of these and thus of extending the network beyond the university itself.
  - Accommodation and residential committees. The chaplain can encourage reflection on pastoral needs, and the relation between pastoral care and discipline.

Departments

The importance of having links with Christians in departments has already been noted.

It is also important to have formal links. Once again this demands chaplaincy links either on a school, faculty or departmental level. At the latter level links can be facilitated by lunch with the head of department. This may only be once a year – but it is about being seen and about communicating the nature of the chaplaincy and how it serves students and staff. Such links ensure that where there are opportunities for collaboration with departments these can be taken up.

The chaplaincy can establish representatives in each department, with the tasks of identifying and communicating important issues, and disseminating information about chaplaincy events. Often key members of departments, especially for pastoral care co-ordination, are support staff such as secretaries or clerks.

Links with staff can also be made through becoming involved in staff development seminars, both as enabler, in areas such as response to student death, and also as co-learner.

Halls of Residence

Halls of residence are important for networking. They form discrete and often very close communities, and appropriate networking can ensure that the chaplain is known by a lot of hall members. Where there is little opportunity to spend time, close contact with the hall warden or hall council will provide a basic link. However there are many ways in which the chaplain can develop this:

- Regular lunch with the wardens.
- An annual pastoral care training session, with warden and sub-wardens from all halls.
- Becoming part of the hall council or governing body.
- Linking in to the Christian Union cell groups based in the hall.
- Linking in to the social side of the hall, including theatrical events and balls.

Student Services

The chaplaincy tends to fall into the student services area. As already noted, for some universities this means that they are managed by the student support manager. For others it means they are part of a looser student support team or network. Some chaplains are ambivalent about being part of such a group, fearing a loss of autonomy.

However, there are great advantages to being a part of this. First, the pastoral stance of the chaplaincy is bigger than simply caring for the Christians on campus. Second, the provision of care for the campus is too big for any one organization. It is important to develop collaboration with the student services not least because of mutual referral. Third, it is important to show how chaplaincy relates to the whole of student support, and this demands dialogue as well as collaboration. This can be seen, for instance, in the chaplaincy working for a community approach to care, as distinct from simply a service approach, and through the development of dialogues that examine spirituality and student care. One chaplaincy, for instance, regularly held a well-attended workshop on spirituality in the annual conference of the student support network. This included spirituality and employability, spirituality and counselling, and spirituality and loss.

A good example of how this comes together with departments and student services is in guidelines for responding to student death, an example of which is given below.

Guidelines for Response to Student Death or Major Crisis

The following procedures have been drawn up to help departments in the event of a student death or major traumatic incident such as a traffic accident, or an attack on a student.

Their aim is to provide a rapid, flexible and sensitive response to major incidents which draws on skills available across the campus and is available at all times.

A coordinating team has been appointed to work closely with senior management, to ensure that guidelines are followed and incidents dealt with as efficiently and effectively as possible. **In the event of such an incident, please contact any member of the co-ordinating team, who will notify all other members**.

The team is:

. . . Head of Student Counselling Service
Telephone:
Email:

. . . Chaplaincy Co-ordinator
Telephone:
Email:

. . . Student Office Manager
Telephone:
Email:

. . . Head of Communications
Telephone:
Email:

Weekends and evenings – please contact Security if a crisis occurs over a weekend or in the evening. They will get in touch with the appropriate members of the Team. The University Security's emergency number is . . .

The guidelines are being circulated to all departments, the Students Union and other campus agencies. For more copies, please contact the University Student Counselling Service reception.

The best place for an initial response is most often the department or agency concerned (such as a Hall of Residence). The Department will often know the student best, and have the best avenues of contact with families and friends.

The Department should, in collaboration with the Coordinating Team:

- Check what other groups might be involved, e.g. Student Union societies.
- Inform students and staff in the Department.
- Be prepared to speak to the media (through the Press Office) if necessary.
- Ensure pastoral support for students and staff.
- Be prepared to meet with the parents and show them round

the Department and make arrangements for the collection of personal effects.

- Liaise with the family and students about the funeral, and possibly arrange transport from the Department.
- Liaise with all concerned groups about any memorial service.

The Co-ordinating Team will:

- Provide a link to the Vice-Chancellor's office and senior management;
- Act as a bridge between the department/agency affected and the range of resources available in the University and beyond;
- Ensure that each incident is effectively followed up;
- Ensure that unnecessary duplication is avoided;
- Respond to requests for help with the costs of accommodating relatives and other incidental costs.

Team members can offer particular support in the following areas:

The Head of the Student Counselling Service

Will offer assistance in counselling students affected by incidents, and by providing information on how staff may access counselling help. He will also be on hand to talk through appropriate responses to difficult situations.

The Chaplaincy Co-ordinator

Will especially advise staff on responding to student death. He will be available to discuss issues such as University attendance at funerals and community remembrance. He will also assist with and, if asked, co-ordinate memorial services. The Chaplaincy will co-ordinate the pastoral and spiritual response of different religious faiths, and directly provide pastoral support as appropriate.

Student Office Manager

This office will co-ordinate responses to legal, financial, insurance and administrative matters, with University and external bodies. It will ensure that all University officers who need to respond are notified. These will include:

- The Vice-Chancellor
- PVC Student Affairs
- The Secretary
- The Academic Registrar
- Security
- Relevant Student Support Network members
- All other relevant offices

In the case of a postgraduate student, these tasks will be carried out in collaboration with . . . of the Research Degrees Office.

Head of Communications

The Press Officer will advise on whether or when public statements should be issued and what they should say. All Press enquiries to Departments should be referred to the Press Officer unless another specific arrangement has been agreed.

Informing the Co-ordinating Team

Information of an incident can reach the University via many points of entry, eg Security, Hall of Residence, Students Union, Academic Department, the Press. Whatever the point of entry, it is important to inform the Co-ordinating Team, who can facilitate a response or help in supporting a response. The Team's contact numbers are listed in the introduction to these guidelines. The appropriate Team members can be contacted at home through Security.

Facilitating the Response

The Co-ordinating Team and Department or Hall of Residence will ensure that family, friends or colleagues are contacted.

Students should be informed of the help that can be provided by the Chaplaincy, Counselling, Student Union Welfare Office, Health Service or any of the other University support agencies.

Alerting relevant agencies within and outside the University

The Co-ordinating Team will ensure that there is a swift and supportive response at all levels of the University, including a letter of condolence from the Vice-Chancellor, the alteration of records in services such as the library and smooth collaboration with external agencies such as the police or, in the case of a death abroad, with any embassy.

Supporting the Response

The Co-ordinating Team will support Departments and Halls in their response to the particular needs of family and friends. Typically, in the event of death, the family will want to come to the University, to the Department, to the flat or Hall of Residence and to pick up the effects of the deceased. The University, through the Co-ordinating Team, may be able to offer accommodation, food and support when this occurs. This could also be provided by the Department.

Funerals

The Chaplaincy can advise in making arrangements for funerals. Wherever possible, a senior Department staff member and/or senior University representative should attend a student's funeral. A Department could also organise transport to allow students to attend the funeral.

After a Funeral

It may be appropriate for some form of community remembrance to take place. Such an act of remembrance may take many different forms, from the planting of a tree to the development of a non-religious service of remembrance, to a full religious memorial service. The Chaplaincy and the

Co-ordinating Team are able to take this on or to assist Departments or Halls in organising it.

International Students

Particular problems may arise with the death of an international student, such as how the body is to be returned home and who is responsible for that. In general, responsibility would fall to the family or Consulate. In exceptional circumstances, the University may be able to help. When in doubt, contact . . . in the first instance.

Summing Up

Every incident of this magnitude will have different needs and will require different particular responses, hence the need for flexible and creative collaboration.

Chaplains have a unique appreciation of the spirituality of death, bereavement and mourning and in particular of associated rituals. However, it is important to note that in any relationship with a department, even where the head is a Christian, there may well be projections on to the chaplain, with the fear of being taken over by a directive clergy-person. The result is the need to negotiate carefully with each new contact, making clear the limitations of the chaplaincy, and to appreciate the central role of the department in this situation. In effect the contract agreed with the institution has to be re-established with each member of the organization the chaplain works with.

Student Union

As noted in Chapter 3 the student union is a complex organization which operates on behalf of the student and at the same time has to be self-financing. A member of the chaplaincy team should be responsible for networking with the union executive committee and the union management team. The executive committee is elected each year, and therefore the chaplaincy team should get acquainted with them as soon as the changeover occurs in August. The executive committee technically appoints the management staff, including the full-time welfare advisor and her office, though they provide the continuity in union business.

It is possible to make many different networks between the union and local churches. Student Action, for instance, runs many volunteers for local projects, who could be used in church projects. Members of the union executive are often involved in community liaison and could link into church networks.

Staff Unions and Human Resources

There are key groups on campus, such as the unions, human resources and occupational health which the chaplain should be aware of and if possible link in with. The easiest route is to become part of any staff support network, and where there isn't one, to help to create it. Such a network would meet perhaps once a semester to share issues and practice.

Conclusion

If worship sets up connections between God and community in context, then networking builds bridges between different communities, Christian and non-Christian, on and off campus.

Networking is central to the mediation of Christian presence on campus. The bigger the network, the more the theology of presence is worked out, and the more the chaplaincy team becomes in reality fully a part of the university and aware of and responsive to all the many different groups who form a part of 'the' university.

Each chaplaincy team needs to carefully work through how the different members develop such networking, which networks are the priorities for them, and which can be maintained with minimum input from the team.

Networking demands attention to both time and place. The rhythm of networking, tying into the university rhythm and the rhythm of the different groups, has to be followed.

Above all networking which is focused on practice facilitates significant ministry, providing the base for prophecy, worship, pastoral care and spiritual reflection, not least through enabling many different narratives to meet and challenge each other. A key part in networking on campus is the development of a website that links into other groups – Christian and non-Christian. There are many resources on campus that can facilitate this.

Finally, such networking is important whether work with students is from a university or local church perspective. Local churches, for instance, need to fit into such a network to enable them to meet the needs of students, especially international students, in the most effective way.

References

Boyce, G., 'Towards a Christian Theology of Multi-faith Tertiary Chaplaincy', *Journal of the Tertiary Campus Ministry Association* 1 (4), 2002.

Gilliat-Ray, S., *Religion in Higher Education*, Ashgate, Aldershot, 2000.

Legood, G., 'Chaplains and the Parochial Ministry', *Contact*, 138, 2002.

Robinson, S., Kendrick, K. and Brown, A., *Spirituality and the Practice of Healthcare*, Palgrave Macmillan, Basingstoke, 2003.

Part 3

Pastoral Work

6

Spiritual and Pastoral Care of Students

The pastoral care of students ranges from care for traditional students, to mature students, to international students. This chapter begins with a definition of spiritual and pastoral care, then moves into the student experience and the nature of faith development. It then examines the pastoral response and particular pastoral issues in the life of the traditional student, such as the development of sexual identity.

The Distinctiveness of Spiritual and Pastoral Care

What makes chaplaincy pastoral care different from counselling or medical care?

It is useful here to quote in part the mission statement of the Association for Pastoral and Spiritual Care (a division of the British Association of Counselling and Psychotherapy):

> Pastoral care happens when representative Christian persons, recognising a transcendent dimension to human life, help others by listening, responding, praying or providing caring support. Pastoral care seeks to foster people's growth as full human beings together with a development of ecologically holistic communities in which all persons may live humane lives. This role can range from sensitive listening and sharing as a friend or neighbour, to specific ministries to people who face crises, traumas, loss or personal dilemmas.

There are certain key points of distinctiveness in pastoral care:

1 Pastoral care has a much more flexible dynamic than counselling. On the whole counselling operates reactively, in response to a request from the client to be seen, and through the development of

a contract. Chaplaincy can operate reactively, interactively and proactively. It can make links with halls of residence and departments which can lead to pastoral care coming up as part of these relationships. Equally, for instance, chaplains can operate in a proactive way at times of student death, going out to family and friends, where appropriate. The counselling approach is built on a view of autonomy that stresses respect for client choice, with the client taking the initiative to seek help. The pastoral care approach majors on the communication of care, which can lead to the chaplain taking the initiative of care.

2 Pastoral care offered by chaplaincy is very much concerned with reflection and the development of spiritual meaning. This may not mean religious meaning per se, but rather significant life meaning. This may be expressed through enabling ritual at times of crisis, or through one-to-one caring, including pastoral counselling, which gives attention to the person's spiritual meaning. None of this demands directive care, in the sense of the chaplain telling the person what to do, believe or value. Rather does it demands reflective care in which the person is enabled to articulate her spiritual narrative, reflect upon it and take responsibility for it (Robinson 2001). It is important to note that secular counselling and psychotherapy do not dismiss or ignore such a dynamic, and that some secular counsellors would have similar aims (Kaufmann 1980).

3 Chaplaincy can both provide a range of care in its team, and also collaborate closely with other support agencies on and off campus. Broadly, either within the team or in collaboration with these agencies the chaplaincy should be able to provide for the student:

- *Pastoral care*, in the form of befriending. Campbell's concept of the skilled companion, used with healthcare workers, could equally apply to this form of care (Campbell 1986).
- *Pastoral counselling*. This form of pastoral care differs from care in general through the intentional setting up of a contract with the student to work through a particular problem or issue (Lyall 1995, Robinson 2001). This is essentially nondirective and would be open to all students.
- *Christian counselling*. In this, the contract for counselling includes explicit reflection on the faith traditions, doctrine and the Bible and includes the possibility of prayer and ritual that would help the Christian to achieve resolution.

- *Community care*, where the community becomes the focus of care. This might be an ordinary Christian community, or a group set up with a therapeutic aim, such as an exam anxiety group.
- *Itinerant care.* This is immediate pastoral care carried out in corridors, departments and the like. It may lead to other longer term expressions of pastoral care, or may be sufficient in itself.

The Student Experience

The student experience is very much about transitions, summed up in the student life cycle of arrival, examinations and endings.

Arrival

One of the biggest transitions is the experience of moving out of home and into university. For many this involves the separations and attachments of late adolescence. The change of environment and all the associated challenges create something of a turmoil, involving feelings of anxiety and insecurity alongside excitement, challenge and stimulus. For many people this will induce initial homesickness. This can easily be underestimated and can affect as much as two-thirds of first-year students (Fisher 1989). Underlying this is grief about the loss of the past and, in particular, childhood. The student cannot go back to where they were, even their room is no longer theirs. This can lead to ambivalent feelings about home and parents. Initially, the chaplain can fulfil the role of temporary support person, allowing the student to grieve and to articulate her story.

A student may find it hard to get out of the grieving process for several reasons, including:

- Major differences between the home environment and university, leading to culture shock. This is seen most clearly in international students. However, moving from a small rural village in the UK to a university of 30,000 people can also be a major shock.
- Lack of skills to develop a new life for oneself. The image of drowning and being unable to swim is quite often communicated.

- Feelings of being marginalized. The student in her previous environment may have been a big fish in a small pool.

Homesickness can, in some cases, last a long time. One student continued to phone her mother twice a day for a year. The chaplain provided a weekly space for her to come and talk, in effect demonstrating that there was someone who she could place her faith in. By the beginning of her second year she was a vital and exuberant part of the medical faculty. The key point at which homesickness might become a major problem is when the student's work or other relationships are being affected and when she exhibits signs of depression, such as lack of concentration, anxiety, disturbed sleep and loss of motivation.

Triggers

The transition from home to university may trigger other problems, including:

- Fear of leaving home because the attachment to parent is felt to be insecure (Heyno 1999).
- The resurfacing of unresolved experiences and problems. In this the transition puts stress on the usually effective coping mechanisms, allowing issues of conflict, anger or low self-esteem to emerge. Some students find experience of bullying or even childhood abuse re-emerging.
- Problems associated with leaving a bad situation at home. Increasingly, for instance, parents who wish to separate choose to do so soon after the last child has left for university. Often the student feels responsible for this, believing that if only he had stayed at home this could have saved the marriage. Other students may feel responsible for leaving behind a single parent who has relied upon them.
- Leaving behind a significant partner. A boyfriend or girlfriend may still be at home or have moved to another university, stirring up many different issues. Some students will go to the extreme of moving university.

Underlying all these factors is the need for the student to do her own work of separation and closure. Related to that is the issue of responsibility and how he can let go of perceived responsibilities and develop others. Where there is a counsellor on the chaplaincy staff they can be available for many of these issues should they appear. Where there are issues of the gravity of childhood sexual abuse, the chaplain should refer the student to student counselling or the student medical practice.

Examinations

The modular approach has made exam anxiety even more intense. Now every semester involves three or more exams. Exam times tend to raise two areas of concern, exam skills and relaxation, and underlying problems triggered by the exam. In the first of these the main aim of pastoral care is to focus on the exam, providing support during the time of stress. This may include relaxation sessions, and helping the student to develop and maintain revision and exam skills. The last two of these may involve referral to exam preparation or anxiety groups, or to the learning and teaching centre.

Like arrival, exam times may trigger underlying problems. Perhaps the commonest is the student who has come to university based on fulfilling his parents' life-script. This can raise debilitating anxiety about failure, leading to depression. For others there may be a sense of underlying anger, fuelled by a resentment of the parents. Others may feel a sense of guilt at achieving success greater than their parents.

Fowler (1996) suggests that behind much of this is perfectionist shame, a sense of intense shame if the person does not live up to the expectations of significant others. This is invariably based on a conditional acceptance of the self, with worth based on achievement. Such a 'script' is, of course, reinforced by the stress at school and university on the importance of individual academic success.

First semester exams can coincide with the 'mid year blues', where the student is in any case tired after the exams, and has lost motivation.

Endings

As the end of life at university looms, similar issues of transition emerge. The loss of university life and the transition to work raises issues of purpose and vocation. For many this is a time of excitement and expectation. Increasingly this area is being addressed from the word go through modules run by the careers' office often in collaboration with departments. One such module looks at theology and employability. This explores what a theology degree has to give to employment, and how different career-relevant skills and qualities might be developed by this. This is often linked to the development of the personal development profile (PDP).

For a small minority of students, though, the imminent end of their academic career sees them still not handling the tasks of adolescence, with even very bright students being brought up short. For some the feeling of adolescence running out is just too daunting. They are not ready to move into the world of work. Others exhibit behaviour quite out of character. Heyno (1999, 35) notes one student who was heading for a 'first' and with a month to go announced to his parents that he was moving in with an older woman, who had two children. The presenting feeling was of romantic love, but in effect he did not want to complete the adolescent tasks, and so simply chose another 'parent'. Some students purposely choose to fail, seeing this as the only way of breaking free from parental expectations.

The chaplain can be a very effective support in these last few months, encouraging the student to take time, and not to make a decision until she has to, and enabling her to critically question the life-scripts placed on her by her parents, without necessarily losing the benefits of the degree.

The underlying dynamic throughout this life cycle is that of late adolescence, summed up in these tasks:

- Separation and independence from parents.
- Development of personal beliefs and attitude.
- Establishing sexual identity.
- Developing the capacity for lasting relationships, which can include expressions of sexual love.
- Developing commitment to life projects, including work.

Stages of Faith

Interwoven with any transition is development of faith, either in the religious sense or in a generic sense of placing faith in significant people, organizations or ideas (Fowler 1996). Such faith may even be the cause of problems experienced by the student, and the development of faith may be crucial to a healthy and creative response. James Fowler proposes seven stages of faith which he locates at different ages:

Fowler's Stages of Faith

Undifferentiated or primal faith (infancy). This is a pre-linguistic and pre-conceptual stage which forms the cradle of trust or mistrust, of self-worth based on unconditional or conditional grounds.

Intuitive-projective faith (ages 2–6). This stage builds upon the development of language and the imagination. With no cognitive operations that could test perceptions and thus reverse beliefs, children grasp experience in and through powerful images. The child is thus attentive to ritual and gesture.

Mythic-literal faith (7–12). This sees a reliance on stories and rules, and the narrative that is implied in the family faith experience. The lived faith of the family – through practice, ritual and belief – is valued in a concrete and literal sense. This can also involve some testing of the story meaning.

Synthetic-conventional faith (12–21). The child in this stage moves on to search for 'a story of my stories'. This looks to the development of life meaning and the person's particular life meaning. At one level this is a product of the development of new cognitive abilities. At the same time the developing life meaning is built up of the original faith system, and thus compiled of conventional elements. This faith is often accompanied by a strong sense of the need to keep together the faith group as a priority.

Individuative-reflective faith (21–30). Faith meaning is more personally chosen and believed. There is an awareness that one's view is different from others, and can be expressed in abstract terms. The faith developed at this stage is for the sake of the person and of making sense of her life in family or community. It is not developed primarily for the unity of the family.

Conjunctive faith (31–40). In this stage many of the different ideas and perspectives, and the resulting tensions and paradoxes are worked at. Previously not examined, these are now held together in balance, with an openness to the perspectives of others. This stage sees a deepening of appreciation of the complex nature of faith and life meaning.

Universalizing faith (40 and beyond). This not so much a stage of faith as a category of individuals who have developed a coherent faith which is grounded in the 'Other', and which enables them to live unfettered by self-concern. Membership of this group is very rare and includes, for instance, Mahatma Gandhi and Martin Luther King.

Criticisms of the stage approach include arguments that it is too cognitive/intellectual, and too individualistic. Others argue that the stages are normative with the later stages seen as superior to the early ones. Yet others question the adequacy of the research (Parks 1992).

However, first, though Fowler sees the stages to be invariant, sequential and hierarchical, in other words they have to be gone through in turn, he does not advocate that they be taken too rigorously. They are a useful tool for noting characteristics of faith development, and which can help the practitioner to be aware of needs. Second, Fowler does argue for a broader rational view of faith including affective, emotional knowledge. The intellectual component of spirituality does not make it a superior form. Third, he argues that the needs expressed in the earlier stages are not left behind. Hence, in times of major crises there is always a felt need to relocate in the most primitive of faiths in some one or being, a perfectly healthy regression.

Fowler suggests that as the person develops new approaches to faith there is a *transition stage* of faith development (Fowler 1996, 71). Based on the work of William Bridges he indicates four interrelated aspects that can make a helpful framework for the chaplain in identifying such a transition phase and accompanying spiritual crisis or pain: disengagement, disidentification, disenchantment and disorientation.

- *Disengagement* involves a major breakdown in some context of relationship and shared meaning that has helped to constitute the sense of self. Extreme examples of this might be divorce, severe illness or leaving home.
- *Disidentification* is the internal element of disengagement. It is experienced as the person tries to rediscover her identity in the old patterns of faith and can no longer identify herself in them.
- *Disenchantment* involves a loss of faith in the old perceptions of reality. This can bring with it feelings of anger and resentment, grief, loss, guilt, shame and confusion. As Fowler notes, 'It can also bring a sense of liberation and empowerment', a sense that there are new and exciting ways of envisioning life and value.
- *Disorientation* is the cumulative effect of the other three stages involving a loss of any sense of direction and a great deal of time and energy spent in trying to grasp what is going on. Bridges refers to this as the neutral zone, a time when the person can feel that they are going out of their mind, and indeed feel that they are no longer 'themselves'.

It is important to note that:

- Transition can lead to a sense of despair and from this to depression.
- This experience is different from clinical depression. It is possible, for instance, in faith transition to retain a sense of humour (Fairchild 1990).
- Such spiritual pain is not bad per se. The disorientation may feel bad but is not necessarily pathological and may lead to growth. This is part of the process that may be termed inversion, as the person looks in towards herself and begins to try to find the resources necessary to face the experience.

At its most extreme this is characterized by St John of the Cross in Christian spirituality as the *dark night of the soul* (Fowler 1996, 74). The classic signs of this experience are:

- A sense of the absence of one's ground of faith.
- A fearful sense of losing some other important foundation point

in ones life, from significant people, to ideals orvalues, to self image, to purpose, or even gratification.

• A sense of sadness about the felt inability to grow spiritually.

For all students these kinds of faith crisis are common in times of transition. A great many students, as noted above, put their faith in ideas or life-scripts which they feel give them value and life meaning, in particular the belief that academic success is critical. This conditional view of faith, 'I am of value if I do well', can become more and more exhausting and difficult to sustain in the light of the competing views of well-being in and around the university. Hence, many students will feel disenchanted with this as a basis for living but unsure about their identity precisely because it has been largely based upon this.

In Christian faith terms students at stage 3 or 4 can feel very threatened. They may have come to university from a home which nurtured a strong basis of faith, only to be faced by many competing views of Christianity. At its most extreme this can lead to anxieties about identifying God's purpose in the student's life and to a sense of paralysis, being unsure as to what God wants and how this might even be identified.

The Pastoral Response

The pastoral care and counselling response can be divided into four stages:

1 *Enabling the student's narrative.* Broadly speaking this allows the student to develop awareness of what has happened and is happening, and how he is feeling, the first step in empowerment. The very act of articulation enables the student to begin to see what she really does feel and think.

2 *Enabling the student to reflect* on the spiritual and moral meaning that is embodied in her story. This might simply involve the chaplain reflecting back to the student the meaning he has heard. It might involve an invitation to the student to say something about how he sees and feels about God, or asking her to say more about any sense of hope she has. One student, for instance, was very fearful of God and could only see him as 'a

pair of glowering eyes viewed through slate grey clouds'. This in turn was reinforced by a strong faith in educational success and by a conditional relationship with parents. Such reflection will also bring to the surface negative feelings about such meanings. One student said that she just wanted some peace; God seemed never to stop 'prying into her soul'.

There may be more than one major conflict of value or life meaning, either within the faith structure or between that and other areas. A typical conflict is between a strong sense of unconditional care for others and a strong sense of conditional care for the self, with the student believing she has to take responsibility for parents and possibly many others. Another common conflict is between a conditional faith, which stresses the need to fulfil standards in order to be accepted by God and the Church, and a conditional student peer pressure, demanding involvement in social groups and cultures in order to feel accepted.

The task of the chaplain is not to resolve such conflicts for the student but to provide a secure environment from which she can begin to explore those contradictions and from there to begin to frame critical criteria, enabling her to question the different grounds of faith. This can feel very scary. Many years of responding to a judgemental God, person or group disempowers the person and doesn't allow them to speak with any frankness of feeling. One student held in her anger with God so much that it would eventually erupt, often with obscene language. This caused her to feel that she had committed a sin against the Holy Spirit and pulled her back into a further cycle of guilt. Hence, the pastoral care relationship has to model and embody the kind of healthy mutual and critical conversation that will allow the person to enter into a relationship with persons, groups or God which is not perfectionist (Robinson 2001).

3 *Developing meaning*. As the meaning is being wrestled with, the student can begin to take responsibility for her own spirituality. Kaufman sees this development of spiritual meaning as at the heart of any therapy (Kaufman 1980). The pastoral care relationship will aim to give the person confidence to develop that spirituality and also embody the basis of an unconditional spirituality, allowing the student to move away from a

dominant conditional spirituality in her faith, work or relationships. Hence, the pastoral relationship will be the basis for any
development in meaning, which is both accepting and challenging, balancing conditional and unconditional acceptance
(Kaufman 1980, 65), and thus developing faith, hope, empathy
and agape (Robinson 2001).

   Sometimes this is seen in Christian terms as a movement from
a literal to a more liberal faith. This is not necessarily the case.
Where a student is having her conditional faith reinforced, albeit
unintentionally, by an evangelical or high church then she may
decide to move to a more liberal church. However, many prefer
to stay in their church and develop their new awareness and
perception in that context, or to be member of more than one
church. This enables continued conversation between different
faith perspectives, and further development. It is important to
note also that this does not encourage the development of a
consumerist approach to faith. Establishing an open and dialogic
relationship with one's faith enables both problems to be seen
clearly and also discernment of vocation in its broadest sense.

4 *Reconciliation and forgiveness.* Finally pastoral care looks to
   enable action, putting into practice the developing meaning.
   This may involve planning that generates further hope, testing a
   relationship to confirm faith or moving into reconciliation and
   forgiveness.

Such an approach is critical to the pastoral integrity of the chaplain
for several reasons:

• It is the most effective in dealing with any projection that might
  be placed on the chaplain. The student, for instance, may view
  the chaplain as an authority figure, and hope that he will take
  responsibility for resolving the problem she has experienced.
  Alternatively he may be viewed as a liberal 'uncle' who will give
  permission for a more relaxed moral code. The person-centred
  approach to pastoral care aims to ensure that over time the student
  takes responsibility for meaning and action, and through that to
  develops autonomy. Hence, it is not the task of the chaplain to
  push the student on to what he sees as a more mature faith, but
  rather to enable her claim and develop her own faith, Christian or
  non-Christian.

• While it is not directive, it does focus on spiritual and moral meaning, and upon a critical engagement with all that has given that meaning. Critical engagement does not necessarily involve leaving any tradition. Indeed, it many strengthen links to these.

- Given that the chaplain is often used by students from many different Christian traditions, this approach ensures that the chaplain is not partial, but rather enables a critical and creative approach to all.

The process is basically the same for all the different kinds of pastoral care, involving the same skills and attitudes. The difference is simply how it is used and in which context. It might be embodied in a pastoral counselling 'contract'. In a student situation this is commonly one of five weeks. The contract can then be reviewed and continued if it is agreed. The process might be embodied in befriending, pastoral support which does not have a structured contract. It can even be offered in more fragmented ways, in corridors or common-rooms. In such situations the student is often looking for space to share feelings, and what might take months in counselling can be addressed in a moment (Nouwen 1994).

The process is also at the heart of the spiritual direction that the chaplain can offer. Once again what makes it different from pastoral counselling is the intention of the relationship. The aim in this is to set up a discipline for spiritual development, enabling the person to reflect on Christian spirituality and how it connects to all parts of her life (Guenther 1992). Similarly Christian counselling aims to work through a problem in relation to the person's spirituality, the Bible and the traditions of the Church.

In addition to such a process the chaplain can develop other resources:

- Spiritual tools such as meditation and relaxation techniques.
- Small groups aimed at exploring faith in a confidential context.
- The conscious use of prayer (Rose 2002). Prayer can be a very important part of care and counselling of Christian students. Clearly, it explicitly involves God in the process. At the same time it models conversation with God which is neither formal nor fearful. Hence, the student will have some experiential sense of what it is to relax or speak plainly with God. The timing of such prayer needs to be negotiated with the student.
- Conscious use of ritual. In one sense, as Legood notes, the chaplain's care is very different from the counselling process

because he has to offer God's forgiveness (Legood 1999). This, of course, depends on the context. For some he will offer the forgiveness of God in and through specific rituals. For others he will seek to enable the person to reflect on relationships such that forgiveness can be sought and accepted. Even for non-Christians this may involve ritual of some kind. Any such ritual seeks to enable an awareness and acceptance of forgiveness.

Particular Pastoral Issues

While in one sense students are no different from others there are particular issues that keep recurring.

Debt

The chaplain should refer students who are unable to handle debt to the student union welfare office, which can work through strategies for dealing with debt. Debt leads for most to the need for paid employment and to greater pressure placed on the student's academic time. The stress caused by debt can also exacerbate the kind of conflicts noted above.

Relationship Problems

A significant number of students find it hard to develop the skills of long-term commitment. This may involve problems with boyfriend or girlfriend or the more mundane problems of how to form friendships or how to get on with flatmates. In the first of these most often the chaplain is consulted about the breakup of a relationship or questioned about how far any sexual relationship should go. In both cases the chaplain can provide the counselling framework noted above.

Some students find making friends so difficult that even going to meals at the hall of residence can seem a major crisis. In such cases the chaplain can work through strategies for making friends, but perhaps above all point the student to an appropriate group, from a therapeutic group to a regular Christian group. Where none exists then again an ad hoc group can be set up. It may be important to continue to provide support or refer them on to student counselling.

Problems with housemates are frequent, and brief support can give the strategies for help. Where necessary the chaplain can provide proactive pastoral care, acting as mediator, providing this is agreed upon by all parties.

Cults

Following up any material on cults produced by the chaplaincy (Chapter 9) some students may come to be helped in leaving cults. The chaplain can put students in touch with agencies described in Chapter 9, or simply work through the pastoral care process, to enable them to take responsibility for exiting the group. In extreme cases the chaplain or other responsible Christian may have to go with the student to effect closure.

Sexual identity

For any student, developing a settled sexual identity is the most demanding maturational task they will face. Some come to a chaplain to explore whether premarital sex is acceptable. One student had a relationship with a non-Christian which was described as the best and most liberating she had ever experienced, and felt that her Christian faith was constraining her. Others come with more extreme problems about how they have avoided real intimacy and commitment in sexual relations. One student had realized that his weekend habits at clubs were developing into predatory behaviour and that he had lost control. He purposely chose a chaplain in order to explore the ethics of his behaviour. Once again it is not the task of the chaplain either to give permission to certain behaviour or to impose, however subtly, a particular moral stance. The task is rather to enable the student to take responsibility for their own spiritual and moral meaning and to enable creative and critical engagement with the different ethical and spiritual narratives which have made up their belief and value systems.

The other major aspect of sexual identity for some students is the emergence of homosexual feelings.

Student A was from an evangelical background which had given him clear indications that homosexuality was a major sin. Since arriving at university two months earlier, he had felt increasingly strong attraction to a male member of his church. They had formed a friendship but he was unable to say how he felt for the first semester. At the beginning of the second semester he had let out how important he was to him, causing the man shock. The friend had gone for advice to the pastor who had arrived the next evening to speak with A and advised that it was important to pray over him.

A felt anxious, confused and guilty.

As in many cases the chaplain was being used because he was not part of the local church set up, and so could provide space for the student to think and feel things through. It is very important not to take such a student in any direction or to confuse the pastoral and spiritual reflection with either moral guidance on the one hand or human and sexual rights issues on the other.

A very useful set of guidelines has been issued by the Association of Pastoral and Spiritual Care for pastoral care of homosexuals. These include:

1 Examine your own assumptions

- Be aware that being gay may not be the problem.
- Be aware that your client may not wish to explore their sexual identity.
- Be aware that a client concerned about same-sex attraction may not be lesbian, gay or bisexual.
- Be aware that roles in homosexual relationships may not run along the same lines as heterosexual relationships.
- Be aware that because a person is married does not mean that they cannot be lesbian, gay or bisexual.
- Be aware that children are in no more danger from homosexual people than from heterosexuals.
- Assume nothing about lesbian, gay or bisexual behaviour.
- Be aware that the client may expect you to be homophobic and may be looking for signs to confirm this.

2 Be self-aware

- Monitor your own response and attitude regardless of your own sexual orientation.
- Be aware that there may be different dynamics to your other counselling relationships.
- Be clear about the limitations of what you can offer.
- Examine your motivation in working in this area.
- Do not impose your own beliefs.
- Do not pressurize someone to change.

3 Respect

- Respect your client's orientation, personal integrity and lifestyle/culture.
- Respect and acknowledge the pain of those who struggle with their orientation when it conflicts with their belief system.
- Respect and acknowledge the capabilities of you client.

Given the importance of this area it is useful to have one member of the team specializing in it, or to have a specialist in the local church who can be referred to. Where underlying psychosexual problems or evidence of child sex abuse emerges, then referral to student health or counselling is important. This does not preclude support of the student alongside such specialist help.

Mental Health Problems

In their resource pack on students and mental health the National Schizophrenia Fellowship (1995) defines mental illness in terms of a continuum, ranging from relatively mild anxiety and frustrations associated with everyday life to severe problems affecting mood and the ability to think and communicate rationally. Two reports in the late 1990s focused on an increase in more severe mental illness amongst students, the need for a whole university response to this, and the moral duty of the university to provide care (Heads of University Counselling Services 1999, Committee of Vice Chancellors and Principals 2000). The reports note research showing that 40 per cent of student respondents were concerned about depression and 23 per cent about anxiety, phobias or panic attacks. Almost 50 per cent were concerned about low self-esteem and lack of confidence. A survey of academic staff at Hull University revealed 35 per cent reporting recent experience of students they felt had mental health problems. Of these, just below a third were characterized as severe.

The chaplain is in one sense part of the whole university response, and given the incidence of mental illness is likely to become involved in pastoral care at some point in different ways:

- Students with a mental health problem may simply drop into the chaplaincy. This may involve students whose delusions have some kind of religious element.
- Students who are being treated by the medical practice may look to, or be referred to, the chaplaincy for support. One postgraduate student suffering from schizophrenia visited a chaplain regularly for a year.
- Religion may be involved in some way in the genesis of an illness, not least through the development of unhealthy guilt (Swinton 2001, Robinson, Kendrick and Brown 2003). The support of the chaplain modelling a healthy response to guilt and related doctrine can be an important part of support.
- The student with the illness may be Christian, and trying to grapple with her faith in this experience.

Response

The chaplain should be aware of the warning signs of mental illness:

- Behaviour that indicates that the student is persistently tense, sad or miserable.
- Loud, agitated, aggressive behaviour.
- Very withdrawn or unusually quiet behaviour.
- Erratic or unpredictable behaviour.
- Unkempt personal appearance, significant weight changes or decline in personal hygiene.
- Deterioration in quality of work, frequently late for or absent from classes, regularly submitting work late, and poor concentration.
- Changes in eating habits or alcohol/substance abuse.

On some occasions the chaplain will be faced by an emergency, including:

• Suicide threats.
• Clear risk of self-harm or harm to others.
• Acute alcohol addiction or substance abuse.
• Students with auditory or visual hallucinations, or severe paranoia.

In such situations the chaplain should aim to persuade the student to go to the medical practice, and best of all take them to the practice. Where the student refuses to go to the medical practice the chaplain should consult with the doctors. In the rare cases of attempted self-harm the chaplain should call the university security service, which can provide support immediately and call the police and ambulance.

The task of the chaplain in any of this is not to diagnose or treat but rather to provide support which enables the student to feel heard and accepted (Swinton 2001). This does not involve 'playing along' with delusions but focusing on the fears behind them, and gently reinforcing reality.

Where the student is being treated successfully and wants to develop their spirituality then the chaplain can help them to reflect on their grounds of faith and develop a new sense of hope.

In addition to the chaplain's support there may be long-term support from Christian groups and congregations. This requires careful handling. One student was successfully treated for schizophrenia. He still had delusions, but was able to handle them, and had communication difficulties. He went to the university chaplaincy Sunday service and was well coped with by the more experienced members and staff. The newer students, especially female, found him very difficult and often would not return. It is important to have a disciplined response to such group work, such as ensuring that experienced group members are with the student, assisting in communication. The group can also explore roles for the student, for instance, in worship.

Suicide

Between 1990 and 1999 there were '1,482 full time student deaths from suicide or undetermined causes in England, Wales and Scotland, 1,111 of males and 371 of females' (Universities UK 2002).

At first sight this seems enormous, and yet it reflects similar rates as the general population. As the Universities UK report into this notes, a proportion of the student body falls into 'groups at relatively high risk of suicide or self harm' (Universities UK 2002, 11). Significant factors of risk include:

- High levels of alcohol consumption (Grant 2002).
- A willingness to talk about suicide and evidence of thought about how this might be achieved.
- Long-term depression and where the student expresses a strong sense of hopelessness.
- A deep indifference to the future and any relationships.
- Volatile mood swings.

The chaplain may well be called out to attempted suicides, especially if she has links with any hall of residences. Her role should be negotiated with the hall wardens. However, the chaplain is well placed to assist in support of staff and students.

Stanley and Manthorpe (2002) note the importance of monitoring those most at risk of suicide. Students who have suffered regularly from depression and who return to university should not, for instance, be placed in new halls of residence where any feelings of isolation might be exacerbated. Good experience of community will be essential for generating a sense of hope.

Self-harm

It is important to distinguish between harm which is the result of anger directed at the self and harm which is generated by attention-seeking. The first of these may not be evident and typically the student will be at pains to cover up such wounds, such as wearing long-sleeved clothes on very hot days. Rana suggests that such behaviour can be seen as reflecting difficulty in handling ambivalent feeling about dependency. In effect this, as well as suicide attempts, can be seen as the result of feeling hopeless at not being able to move away from parents (Rana 2000, 154). The student is caught in the isolation between home and work, not able to move away or start anew. Once again the chaplain can offer spiritual support in the broader sense, helping the student to identify areas of hope.

Attention-seeking self-harm is very effective in drawing in

members of student groups or housemates. The chaplain may well get a visit from a housemate who has been up more than one night in response to this. It is possible to work together with counselling and accommodation to support the housemates and provide the most effective support for the student who is harming herself.

Student Death and Bereavement

The ultimate transition is death, and it is at university where many first lose someone of significance in their lives. The actual death of a student is not as rare as might be imagined. In some big UK universities there may be as many as ten deaths in any year – not uncommon out of a population of 20–30,000 largely young people.

For the families there is not just the agonizing loss of a child or sibling, but also the fact that the death is most likely to be sudden and traumatic, and in most cases will have occurred many miles away from home. For parents especially, the experience of student life is an odd hinterland. The son or daughter is in a temporary world, away from home yet happy to be home at intervals, independent yet financially dependent, no longer part of that group, yet not settled into precisely where she wants to be.

For many bereaved parents then there is a sense of not quite knowing where their dead child is at rest (Robinson 2002). For the student who has lost a lover, friend or housemate, things can be equally confusing. This is most often the first loss of any kind. Reactions tend to be fearful at the intensity of the grief. Many fear that they are losing control. The stages identified by Kubler-Ross (1972) can be intensified within student groups: shock, disbelief, anger, bargaining, depression, resolution. Where one student died in his year abroad this left a cohort of 20 or more who for two days focused their anger on the university and any representatives who came out. For many there can be further anxiety about how the experience of bereavement might affect their academic perform ance. While many may begin to address the feelings of surrounding grief, for most there is little sense of what mourning is, or the power and need of ritual. Still less have they a sense of how their culture deals with or makes sense of death. Student life in many respects epitomizes the postmodern era, with a stress on the individual's personal narrative, a culture which is very fragmented, and profound cynicism about any overarching narratives that claim a privileged status. Hence, as noted in Chapter 5, it can be important to develop a memorial service which enables students to find meaning through dialogue.

The experience of friendship at university, already a time of transition, tends to be very intense. However, like many parents there is often a difficulty in knowing where to 'place' the deceased. There is little appreciation of their home life and little sense of their life beyond the particular group they belonged to. Hence, for many friends bereavement might lead to a real learning about their friend. Such elements as these are, of course, there alongside the usual feelings surrounding bereavement, not least the sense of guilt if the person has died in a traumatic way.

Chaplaincy response to student death embodies an interactive approach, and might include the following:

- Visiting the friends of the dead student. It is important to have agencies available for the bereaved to come to. However, offering only this kind of reactive care can easily medicalize the experience of bereavement. For male students especially, who often find difficulty in articulating emotions, going to counselling can be seen as a loss of control or a failure. It is more important in early stages then to enable reflection amongst the friends in their home environment.
- Offering the possibility of a formal reflection or debriefing to the student's cohort, enabling them to go through all the facts of the incident and then the emerging feelings. This is best done with another person such as the counsellor. This can be very effective where the death has been traumatic for the whole cohort, such as a suicide.
- Co-ordinating the care of the parents at the university. This may involve being with them as they empty the flat. In the case of parents of international students it can involve several days of pastoral care. Once more this requires working with other support agencies on campus.
- Attending the funeral is important. The chaplain might simply be there and make links with staff, students and family, or might be involved in the service itself.
- Co-constructing a memorial service or event. The process is described in Chapter 5.

Pastoral Care and the Family

Inevitably there are occasions where parents become involved or want to become involved in any pastoral crisis. They may phone up the chaplaincy to say that their son or daughter is having trouble or has not been in touch for some time. Guidelines in such a situation are straightforward:

- It is important not to allow the parents to make use of the chaplain. Data protection legislation means that no information can be passed back to them without the permission of the student. Moreover, it is bad dynamics if the chaplain is seen by the student as an extension of the parent.
- Where the parent is very anxious it is reasonable to give them space to talk and reflect. Most parents are glad of anyone in the university who will attend to their anxieties. Where a student has become part of a cult the chaplain might spend some time enabling parents to think through the dynamics of their relationship and the dynamics that should be avoided if they wish to regain trust. The basis of those is that the parents should respect the student's freedom to make his own choice, and at the same time they should clearly articulate that, while they disagree with them, they are still available for them. Hence they can model a relationship which gets away from the polarizing attitudes of the cult. This does not mean that parents should not demonstrate what the consequences of their choice might be for the future.

  One mother when hearing that her son had decided to move in with a cult said to him, 'It's your choice and we always be here for you. However, in the light of you finding a permanent place we are letting your room out, and we would like you to give us warning when you want to visit, as we do not want you to arrive when we have friends here and start trying to convert them.' The son left the cult three weeks later.
- The chaplain could get in touch with the student, provided that it is clear that he is simply passing on the fact that the student's parent phoned. It is then the right of the student not to get back in touch with parents.
- Where there is the possibility of some harm to the student, or other, then it is important that the chaplain or another pastoral carer should visit.

In the event of student death parents are properly part of the chaplain's care. As noted above this may involve being available when they visit campus and helping them to become involved in memorial services. While pastoral care should be referred to the local minister after this, there are situations in which parents continue to 'touch base' pastorally for many years. All this can be helped by memorials, such as a tree, an annual card sent to the parents or keeping a memorial book.

At key points the deceased student's peers will pay a significant part in the pastoral care of the parents. The primary focus of this is where the parents are trying to learn more of the life of their son or daughter at university (Robinson, Kendrick and Brown 2003). This is worth monitoring by the chaplain as some parents can 'hang on' to the friends, in effect to keep alive their child. This can be difficult for the students.

Community Care

In addition to any one-to-one pastoral care the chaplaincy can provide or link into community care which helps answer pastoral needs before crises emerge. It can pick up the support role of the family, with the worship community providing hospitality and care. One chaplaincy, for instance, advertised a 'homesickness lunch' in intro-week, and was amazed to find over 200 first-year students turning up.

As noted, support groups can be organized for particular groups of students, such as international students, and these can involve local church volunteers. Networks of care expand further through connections with halls of residence and the other care agencies on campus. Pastoral care can be closely related to academic work, especially with the development of courses that stress reflection and connection to life skills and employability, and the personal development profile. One chaplaincy organized a successful half-day on vocation, in the broadest Christian sense, with the careers centre. Links into the academic departments, especially with personal tutors, will also assist pastoral work.

Use of emails is developing as a method of pastoral contact. Pioneered by the Samaritans and Student Nightline, anecdotal evidence suggests that it can be very useful in establishing a pastoral link, which can then be followed up person-to-person. Male students especially seem to use this method, being reluctant actually to visit a chaplain or counsellor. It is important for this that any website should be pastorally friendly. Email is also a useful pastoral link for language students in their year abroad. All this extends the idea of a pastoral community even further.

Reflective Pastoral Practice and Training

As pastoral care is available on the campus it is important to have clear guidelines that can be shared with other agencies and the academic institution. A good example of guidelines are those set out by the Association of Pastoral and Spiritual Care. These articulate goals and values, guidelines for the safety of the 'client' and the pastor, and on confidentiality and competence. They demonstrate how values and goals link into practice, show how the practice is carried out, and demonstrate a clear level of professional competence and reflective practice.

Also important in the team context is clarification of how the team works pastorally, setting out standards and protocols. At one level this is about ensuring an effective pastoral service. This can include the discipline of recording major pastoral contacts and logging in a central book where the student seems at risk, clear understanding of grounds for referral, and regular opportunities for the team to reflect on recent pastoral engagements, through the provision of supervision, individual or group (Foskett and Lyall 1988). Regular pastoral care training can take place in house, together with other members of the student services, or as part of the university staff development programme. As noted above, different approaches to ecclesiology and pastoral theology should not preclude good pastoral teamwork. The ministry of healing, for instance, can be valued by the team, and set out as part of a protocol. This might advocate not using the ministry in the first few pastoral encounters, when a pastoral assessment is being made. After consultation with another member of the team the ministry might be used in the most appropriate context, be that in worship or in a pastoral context. It is important that the rest of the team know when such a ministry is being used, not least because it may well raise interest on campus leading to inquiries.

Conclusion

Pastoral care of students differs very much from traditional parish pastoral care, not least in the focus on individual and group transition. Where possible the chaplaincy should attempt to offer the full range of pastoral care, from counselling to befriending to hospitality and group support, something only possible with an effective team and with good working relations with campus agencies and local churches.

References

Bridges, W., *Transitions: Making Sense of Life's Changes*, Addison Wesley, Reading, Mass., 1980.

Browning, D., *Religious Ethics and Pastoral Care*, Fortress, Philadelphia, 1983.

Campbell, A., *Rediscovering Pastoral Care*, DLT, London, 1986.

Heads of University Counselling Services, *Degrees of Disturbance – The New Agenda*, London, 1999.

Fairchild, R., 'Sadness and Depression', in Hunter, R. (ed.), *Dictionary of Pastoral Care and Counselling*, Abingdon Press, Nashville, 1990, pp. 1103–6.

Fisher, S., *Homesickness, Cognition and Health*, Lawrence Erlbaum Associates, Hove, 1989.

Foskett, J., and Lyall, D., *Helping the Helpers: Supervision and Pastoral Care*, SPCK, London, 1988.

Fowler, J., *Faithful Change*, Abingdon, Nashville, 1996.

Grant, A., 'Identifying Students' Concerns', in Stanley, N. and Manthorpe, J. (eds), *Students' Mental Health Needs*, Jessica Kingsley, London, 2002, pp. 83–106.

Guenther, M., *Holy Listening*, DLT, London, 1992.

Committee of Vice Chancellors and Principals, *Guidelines on Student Mental Health Policies and Procedures in Higher Education*, London, 2000.

Heyno, A., 'Cycles of the Mind', in Lees, J. and Vaspe, A. (eds), *Clinical Counselling in Further and Higher Education*, Routledge, London, 1999, pp. 26–38.

Kaufman, G., *Shame the Power of Caring*, Schenkman, Washington, 1980.

Kubler-Ross, E., *On Death and Dying*, Tavistock, London, 1972.

Legood, G., 'Universities', in Legood, G. (ed.), *Chaplaincy*, Cassell, London, 1999, pp. 132–42.

Lyall, D., *Counselling in the Pastoral and Spiritual Context*, Open University Press, London, 1995.

National Schizophrenia Fellowship IRISS Project, *Students and Mental Health Resource Pack*, National Union of Students, London, 1995.

Nouwen, H., *The Wounded Healer*, DLT, London, 1994.

Parks, S., 'Fowler Evaluated', in Astley, J. and Francis L. (eds), *Christian Perspectives on Faith Development*, Gracewing, Leominster, 1992.

Rana, R., *Counselling Students*, Macmillan, Basingstoke, 2000.

Robinson, S., *Agape, Moral Meaning and Pastoral Counselling*, Aureus, Cardiff, 2001.

Robinson, S., 'Thanks for the Memory . . . Death of a student: Memorials, mourning and postmodernity', *Contact*, 138, 2002, pp. 16–25.

Robinson, S., Kendrick, K. and Brown, A., *Spirituality and the Practice of Healthcare*, Palgrave Macmillan, Basingstoke, 2003.

Rose, J., *Sharing Spaces? Prayer and the Counselling Relationship*, DLT, London, 2002.

Stanley, N. and Manthorpe, J., 'Responding to Student Suicide', in Stanley, N. and Manthorpe, J. (eds), *Students' Mental Health Needs*, Jessica Kingsley, London, 2002, pp. 243–60.

Swinton, J., *Spirituality and Mental Health Care*, Jessica Kingsley, London, 2001

Universities UK, *Reducing the risk of student suicide*, UUK, London, 2002.

7

Staff, Postgraduate and Non-traditional Students

There is a vision of HE chaplaincy that still predominates for many. The chaplain, it seems, works throughout the semester and then once the students leave at the end of June has a wonderful time off to relax and read and write, until mid-September. This is not to mention the four weeks off at Easter and the three weeks off at Christmas.

This, of course, is very far from the truth. While the undergraduates leave for long holidays, the postgraduates remain throughout the year. It also leaves the people who live locally, especially the non-traditional students who have come in through widening participation, and who are struggling to maintain what is either a return to university or a new experience. It leaves groups such as the nurses who have a year-round presence dictated by their profession. It also leaves the international student population who have nowhere to go. Last but not least it leaves the staff.

Even in a student-centred ministry, the staff is a critical part of the student's learning and social environment. Personal tutors, support staff, administrators and so on, all form the social environment within which students are cared for. Hence, a concern for the pastoral care of staff comes with the territory of chaplaincy.

This chapter begins with thoughts about the pastoral care of staff, and then considers postgraduate and non-traditional students.

Staff

As Gordon Graham notes, a new era was ushered in for staff in the 1980s (Graham 2002, 13). Prior to this, academia was seen to be secure, with tenure being the norm and not too stressful. The change of culture has been massive, leading to major stress among the staff:

- With the introduction of the Research Assessment Excercise the pressure is now on staff to produce a minimum of four publications each year. For many staff there is a feeling that this is squandering quality for quantity. In former times a scholar could take a long while to produce a quality publication, now there is not that time for painstaking research.
- Quality control in teaching has generated more administration, and for some has meant a complete reworking of their teaching style.
- The additional administration load in overseeing registration, examinations, student retention and so on has grown with the need to attract more students.
- The increase in students has seen further attention to pastoral care of students, leading to the development of personal tutors. This has led to some staff being overloaded by students with problems. The dynamic in many departments is that those staff who show interest in the students will end up with students at their door. Hence, for many there is a reluctance to get involved in pastoral care.
- The focus increasingly on transferable skills requires more time to factor this into modules.
- With tenure eroding, many staff have had the added pressure of fixed-term contracts. The more the fixed-term contract predominates, the more the staff member feels she has to focus purely on her work to justify her position.

Culture of Change

After an initial burst of change in the 1980s and 1990s, it was hoped by many that a pattern of stable activity could return. This is not the case. Due to continued pressure from government, all universities have moved into a mode of continual change. This applies to all members of staff:

- Student services, such as the library, continually need to respond to student needs, with the ethos of customer care predominating. This leads to the classic stressor of having to handle the change, often major changes within or between sites, and at the same time maintain a service.

- Estates services continually have to juggle space and needs on campus, and place this in a building programme.
- Central administration presides over a cycle of major events, including registration and graduation. These add their own deadline pressures to all the changes.
- Catering and residential staff have been under pressure to stay solvent, through increasing conference trade, and improving services for students and staff.

Such a culture produces major stress, the symptoms of which include:

Muscular tension	Depression
Colds or other illnesses	Anger
High blood pressure	Anxiety
Indigestion	Feeling overwhelmed
Ulcers	Mood swings
Disturbed sleep	Forgetfulness
Fatigue	Unwanted or repetitive thoughts
Headaches	Difficulty concentrating
Irritability	

O'Neill (2002) also argues in the Reith lectures that the pressures in university life, as elsewhere, can erode critical values and attitudes, in particular trust. Such pressures then do not just cause ill feeling, they eat away at shared meaning and value.

Universities, however, should not be seen as simply pathogenic. A great many of the changes have led to the development of genuinely good values and practices, including transparency and reflective practice. A good deal of the pressure has led to creative and healthy stress. Moreover, there remains at the heart of the university staff a strong sense of the significance of HE and ultimately of a spiritual meaning at the heart of the university.

In research conducted by the Leeds Church Institute, the University of Leeds was one of eight organizations where up to 30 staff were interviewed about their spirituality at work (Randolph-Horn and Paslawska 2002). Most of the staff were concerned, in one way or another, about change and the rate of change. Some reported that they had initially feared that the changes had been radically affecting the ethos of the university. This ethos was seen in terms of service to the community and self-evident value of research and teaching and learning. Several staff, however, felt that despite the radical nature of the change the core values had survived. One used the evocative image of the university as the Titanic, which he thought was sinking, with him and the rest of the staff in lifeboats. Turning round to look, it was clear that it was not sinking and they had to row like fury to get back on board. There was a strong sense of faith transition in this image. The change led to many things that were new and challenging, but there could be renewed and different faith in the institution and the community.

This research reinforces the point that spirituality and value are at the heart of work and thus at the heart of any pastoral care of those who are in work. The response of the chaplaincy to staff can be divided into two: reactive work, with those staff who want to use the chaplain, and proactive work, which seeks to provide pastoral and spiritual support for staff in the workplace.

Reactive Response

Chaplaincy is increasingly used by staff for pastoral care, not least because chaplains are seen to be outside the university hierarchy. The following examples illustrate different pathways.

Middle manager A came to the chaplaincy with signs of extreme stress. The major problem was that his university managers gave him far too many tasks. Because of all the changes and uncertainty about his job as office manager, he did not feel able to say no. The result was massive overwork. The chaplain was able to help him gain a better perspective on the issues, not least in terms of thinking through his role in the stress reactions. The staff member had initially come to try to get support in fighting the higher management. It emerged in the further reflection that there was a knock-on effect on his staff. They also were being put under immense pressure. At times of major crisis they would be working seven days a week, and he would give them unrealistic deadlines. In effect, the man who was being abused by his managers was abusing his staff. As this emerged, with its complexities and contradictions, he was able to reflect on underlying contradictions. He was a strong Christian, but tended to keep his faith very private, not applying it to work or getting any sense of spiritual identity from work. A explored the implications of this and began to look at how he might change relationships at work, and how fences had to be mended with his staff.

The spirituality at work research noted how those with a strong Christian spirituality often failed to connect this with work, either in the sense of applying values or of developing an awareness of work as part of God's relationship and his purposes. Hence, with Christian members of staff who come with pastoral problems, part of the response is to enable them to make connections and see how this might affect their practice at work.

> Burn-out from stress is not an uncommon problem for academic staff. This can often focus on the felt need to keep producing and the feeling of the high-flyer when he simply stops producing world-class research. This will often present itself in terms of depression and extreme anxiety. One quite new researcher came to a chaplain, referred by another member of staff. She was very distracted and anxious, clearly wanting to share what seemed a major problem. Each time she was about to share it she shouted, 'No, I cannot tell you. If I tell you I will let go and then I will never be able to finish this work.' The chaplain suggested that she might consider letting go just in the context of their session and move back to research mode as she left. She replied, 'You don't understand, this research is my life, if I allow anything to get in the way of it I am lost.'

At the heart of such problems is the identification of the self with the research, hence if it is either interrupted or is falling away then this is a threat to the very self. Clearly, it is appropriate to offer referral to the staff counsellor or to occupational health. For some, however, anything provided by the university is seen as a threat, leading to this episode going on file. Hence, it would be important to continue with support and where appropriate suggest agencies off campus.

Whatever the course of action, there is need to allow the staff member to re-examine what is essentially her ground of faith, without losing the sense of identity that is attached to success.

In both the previous cases, change in the workplace had exacerbated an underlying problem. For many staff members change itself is the problem. This has been especially so for those over 50 and who the university has encouraged to take early retirement. This forces a fundamental review of their purpose and sense of worth. This requires reflection on faith and grounds of faith, possibly enabling the staff member to find different grounds. Pastoral care in collaboration with human resources can lead to very creative results. One person took early retirement and took up the post of a voluntary missionary, at the age of 53. For him this was the final liberation from his parents' expectations.

Staff Death

Increasingly universities are developing protocols to respond to in-service death. As with students, the chaplain has much to give to that response, not least in possibly making links with the family. Where appropriate memorial services can also be arranged for retired staff who have died. Each memorial service is a chance to rehearse the basic values and different life narratives.

Personal and Faith Issues

Some members of staff, like students, will use chaplains to talk through faith issues away from their home or home church.

For many members of staff who use the chaplaincy in this way there is a sense of spiritual exhaustion and lack of hope. The chaplain's task is to enable the person to locate hope, and to rediscover energy. This might require a range of pastoral care, including simply relaxation and one-to-one meditation.

Proactive services

In close collaboration with human resources (HR), occupational health and staff unions, the chaplaincy can provide pastoral and spiritual resources to staff and even contribute towards the development of the organization's spirituality (Hawkins 1991). This might involve several things including:

- Input to building planning such that quiet rooms can be located at appropriate places around the campus. It is important to locate these in areas where there is a clear community and thus where the culture of using quiet rooms can be modelled and developed. When one quiet room was developed it was hardly used, largely because many staff resented their fellows taking out time to use it. Significantly, there was not the same reaction when it came to cigarette breaks.

- Working closely with human resources, chaplaincy can offer meditation sessions and retreats as part of staff care. The importance of working with HR is in enabling the staff to attend such events without losing pay. Meditation sessions can be made available over lunch-times or half-days. Retreats can vary from half a day to a day during the week. Offered to the whole staff these can focus on spirituality as a generic idea, enabling reflection and meditation. Retreats can also be offered to the Christian staff. Some chaplaincies offer this over a weekend. It is also possible to have meditation aids, such as the labyrinth, mentioned in Chapter 5, available to staff on a regular basis, outside worship.

- Mediation. Chaplains can offer a mediation service to staff where human resources feed unable to do this. Again the position outside the hierarchy enables this.

- Student crises and death can have a major effect on the academic department. The chaplain can offer one-to-one pastoral care but also has the chance of helping departments through leading a debrief, either for the whole department or for the staff who have been responsible for the response to the crisis. Debriefing does not hold any of the possible stigma attached to counselling or after-care. It can be seen to be part of the proper professional response to crisis. The key point about a debrief is that it goes through the basic stages of reflection, and should allow all members to go through each stage together (Parkinson 1993, 167). Anger about the institution can be safely ventilated as part of such groups and lead to changes in practice.

- Regular staff support. Some universities use chaplains to chair monthly debriefing of members of the student support services team. This is ongoing reflection that allows the members to raise issues which cause them difficulty and work through how they might respond, with no manager present. Other chaplaincies host staff 'stress groups', where staff are invited once a month to just talk to each other about the pressures. This is not a 'grumble group' but one which focuses on practice, feelings and action, and explores ways in which a professional relationship can be developed. These are good examples of the chaplain being most effective because she is not part of the hierarchy. In both cases, it is appropriate to explore underlying spirituality.

- Proactive pastoral care for staff should as far as possible be inclusive. From one perspective this means working with unions and making clear that the chaplain is available to all staff. One union, for instance, aims to hold an annual service for those who have died at work. This is something that can be provided by chaplaincy as part of overall care. From another perspective, it means being concerned about managers and heads of the university.
- Generating research on spirituality at work. Such research can get large numbers of staff involved in reflection and raise issues for what might be made available for staff.
- Developing Christian staff groups to enable peer support, and reflection on work and faith.

Postgraduate Students

The life of a postgraduate student can be very problematic:

- Some simply use postgraduate studies to put off the evil hour of having to work through the tasks of late adolescence.
- Some use the postgraduate experience to take their relationship to the parental life-scripts further. For some this involves a desire to please their parents and achieve ultimate success. For others there can be unconscious questioning of that dynamic. One MA student recovering from an eating disorder, focused on trying to gain control from her parents, chose to return to HE. She felt that she had sorted out her problems, and yet chose a subject which she was not good at and which caused her a great deal of anxiety. She had unconsciously locked back into the dynamic of pleasing her parents by achieving success in the most difficult subjects. This was in turn reinforced by a Roman Catholic faith that was strong on guilt. Her dynamic with the staff betrayed a projection of feelings about her parents. They were disapproving. The response of the chaplain had to be reasonably quick, given the MA time-frame. He provided space for her on a fortnightly basis to explore her feelings. At the same time he suggested that she call on the head of department and share her fears. The head happened to be

a good Christian, and he listened carefully to her, before inviting her round to his home for family tea. This was such a surprise to her that it was the beginning of her radically questioning her previous life-script. The chaplain in this case had to stay with her and help to focus on a longer-term approach in which her spirituality could catch up with her therapy.

- A key problem for most PhD students is isolation. Some, especially in the sciences will find that they work in labs alongside other researchers, forming a small community. In other areas the researcher will tend to work for long periods by herself and later subject her work to other researchers or supervisors.
- Identity. The postgraduate is neither student nor fully accepted teacher, though he is in the world of both. In some departments he is not welcome in the junior common room, and only welcome in the senior common room when there are no senior staff around.
- Purpose. At some point many postgraduates begin to question the whole point of the exercise. For many this begins when their expectations are no longer matched by reality. They may doing very sound work, but work that will not get them the top job they wanted or the lifestyle they had hoped for. Once again, vocation and life-scripts begin to be tested.
- Problems with supervisors. The postgraduate student is entirely reliant upon the supervisor. For some, she may not be the right person, and a poor dynamic can quickly develop. Students often feel that if they have got a bad supervisor they can't survive. This is a common problem for international students.

There are three major points of anxiety for the PhD student. First, at the end of the first year there is an upgrading from what is in effect a probationary year to the full PhD. This can be traumatic for some students. Second, in the middle of the three years for a PhD (four or five part-time), there is commonly depression and anxiety. This is almost like hitting the wall in the marathon. The student feels exhausted and demotivated, and can't see how she can last the rest of the time. Third, the final viva examination provides the greatest source of anxiety. Contrary to some views the outcome of vivas are not assured and where the student either fails or is asked to do extensive work on the thesis this can be very traumatic.

Response

The chaplain can respond to postgraduate concerns in several ways:

- One-to-one care and counselling, not least to provide a stable point during the major time of anxiety.
- Work closely with any support that is provided for postgraduates. Many universities do not have support in place for the postgraduate student, in which case the chaplain would be in a good position to work for some. There is usually a postgraduate representative council, made up of students, which the chaplain can at least make a link with. Such a council, locally and nationally, often tries to define the needs of postgraduates carefully with the aim of getting the university to help. Some universities have responded with the development of a graduate centre. This aims to provide a community for postgraduates. If the graduate centre is part of a student support network then chaplaincy can relate to it through the network.
- Chaplaincy can run specific postgraduate groups, from faith to support groups. Sometimes these are run with staff Bible studies. Many Christian postgraduates first come to undergraduate groups, such as SCM, but soon find they do not fit in. It is possible in some chaplaincies to use postgraduates in key support posts, akin to part-time chaplaincy assistants.

Non-traditional Students

The non-traditional student is the one who does not fit into the traditional pattern of a student. They are mature, will often have responsibilities with families, may be part-time and have a job, and may come from lower socio-economic groupings. Some of the more recent universities now have a majority of such students. Indeed, one university has 75 per cent, leaving the more traditional students feeling more marginalized.

For the non-traditional student the experience of HE can be a major challenge. Three brief cases illustrate different extremes.

A man in his early forties was made redundant. He chose to do a self-financed taught MA in social sciences. From the beginning he experienced very negative reactions from the course cohort. He was very different, with more enthusiasm, greater experience of group work, a good seminar style and very different cultural and political views from the other students. Soon the group looked to oust him, treating him with ridicule and undermining his presentations. They then pressurized the staff to have him removed, because they said that his influence was disrupting the class. The teaching staff found themselves unable to cope with this situation and eventually the student was advised to leave, having sought help from the student union, counselling, chaplaincy and solicitors. In the end the student left, and continued for some time to experience traumatic effects, including flashbacks.

(Reported in Lago and Humphrys 1999)

A mother of two with severe dyslexia was accepted at university A. She lived in a difficult area and both children were suffering behaviour problems, including truancy. The mother found learning very hard, not least because she found it very difficult to take advantage of the help offered by the disability office. The problems with her two children caused her to feel guilty. She felt that her being away at university was contributing to their behaviour. She eventually took a year out of her course, but never returned.

Trish was a strong Christian who decided to return to university with her two sons now aged 10 and 12. University life was immensely exciting and extended her beyond her family and previous church life. She met a fellow part-time MA student, the two fell in love and came to see the chaplain in a state of anxiety and depression. There was only two months to go in the degree and she felt that she wanted to leave her husband and begin a new life with the man she loved.

While these three cases may seem extreme, at different times they came across the chaplain's desk. They illustrate some of the key problems experienced by mature students:

- Many mature students see the experience of HE as a major life-changing experience, fuelled by emotional and financial investment.

- Some see it as a way out of certain things – an unsatisfactory marriage, poverty and so on. This can be all the more problematic for students who graduate well but who do not then get the employment they had hoped for.
- The change to formal HE can be both a cultural and learning shock, as the first two cases showed. Access courses are designed to help people into the HE experience, but even these can be problematic as they are usually student-centred, while many university courses are centred in the discipline.
- The fear of failure can loom large for people who everyone assumes are adult and therefore should not have any intellectual problems. The investment in time and energy is such that failure can generate shame for the mature student.
- The person might well come with personal problems which are already deep seated. The converse of this is that many will come who are emotionally mature and thus able to handle possible difficulties.
- Financial sacrifice can reinforce a sense of guilt in the student. Sacrifice of time and attention lead to other members of the family feeling left out and left behind. In the second case, the sons were unhappy to lose their mother to HE, and also to necessary part-time employment.
- The challenges of freedom and a very different culture and values can cause the mature student to question previous values and previous belief systems.

In many ways, this is still very much pastoral care for those experiencing major transitions. However, because of the investment in life up to this point a sense of change can be very traumatic. Major problems that have been dormant for many years may surface because of the pressures of academic or new-found freedom, leading to crisis and change in long-term relationships.

The chaplain can be used very much as support in this area while the student works through questions about her value system. In the first two cases the chaplain was chosen as the end of the line, the students having been to other agencies who could not help, for many different reasons. In case three, the chaplain was chosen because the woman was still convinced about the Christian faith but did not trust her local minister not to lecture her, or to put in jeopardy the freedom and the sense of well-being that she had been discovering outside the church community. The chaplain can help the person identify the values and responsibilities in the church community, in her family and in the new relationship, and then to take responsibility for these in practice.

Response

Very often, there is not the specialized collaborative care that is there for the other students. However, a number of universities are now appointing advisors to mature students. Others are developing support groups which help the transition. There are mature student societies in the student union, but these have a record of starting off well and nose-diving before the end of the first semester. The average non-traditional student does not have the time and energy to maintain a support group. Hence, a member of staff is needed to provide the support and continuity for such a group.

Chaplaincy support, apart from pastoral care and counselling, can aim to:

- Provide Christian support groups, possibly linking in with local church strategies for training.
- Link in with local clergy to raise their awareness of the stress experienced by non-traditional students, and encourage support structures for any such student in the parish.
- Link in with the different support groups on campus.

Conclusion

Work in these three areas can be quite distinct, taking the chaplain's role beyond that of caring for the traditional student. How this is to be achieved depends on the team and other persons available. A part-time member of the team who has had postgraduate experience, for instance, would be able to focus on postgraduate and/or mature student work. It might involve visiting the graduate centre once a week for coffee, making networks with the postgraduate representative council and the officers in charge of the centre. As the networks are built up, then Christians will be identified, who might form the basis for a postgraduate group or take on a link role with the chaplain.

References

Graham, G., *Universities: The Recovery of an Idea*, Imprint Academic, Thorverton, 2002.

Hawkins, P., 'The Spiritual Dimension of the Learning Organisation', *Management Education and Development* 22 (3), 1991, pp. 172–86.

Lago, C. and Humphrys, N., 'Issues of difference in further and higher education', in Lees, J. and Vaspe, A., *Clinical Counselling in Further and Higher Education*, Routledge, London, 1999.

O'Neill, O., *The Reith Lectures 2002*, *www.bbc.co.uk/radio4/reith2002*.

Parkinson, F., *Post-Trauma Stress*, Sheldon Press, London, 1993.

Randolph-Horn, D. and Paslawska, K., *Spirituality at Work Report*, Leeds Church Institute, Leeds, 2002.

8

International Students

If the *Guardian* is to be believed (Robinson and Benwell 1999) then chaplaincy to Higher Education is fast declining and the only real 'customers' are international students. Many international students, it is argued, come to university with the expectation that chaplaincy will provide care and support. They come with traditional church expectations, and often directed by their home pastors to the chaplaincy.

Such an argument ignores the many aspects of wider chaplaincy work and assumes a church model of chaplaincy. Nonetheless, many international students do gravitate to the chaplaincy. For some international students, especially those who can expect international continuity such as the Roman Catholics, it is natural to use chaplaincy as their base. For the most part, however, international students are a very mixed and complex group, with many different expectations and needs.

They are also increasingly a significant percentage of the student population. In 2000 over 313,000 international students entered Britain, with almost 100,000 on postgraduate courses. This compares to just over 200,000 in 1990.

The top five non EU countries from which international students came were the USA, China, Malaysia, Hong Kong and Japan. The top five EU countries were Greece, Germany, France, Eire and Spain. The top three areas of study were business and administration, engineering, and social and political sciences.

The rise in the number of international students is due to some key factors:

- The high reputation of British Higher Education.
- The opening up of communist and former communist states, particularly China to the West.

- The increased mutuality and exchange in the EU. The ERASMUS Programme, enabling study abroad, for instance, was set up in 1987.
- The importance of the English language to global communication, and thus for jobs. In 1998 it was estimated that over 750,000 international students took short English language courses in Britain.
- Higher Education in Britain has become increasingly globalized, developing links with international universities and sometimes setting up departments in other countries.

Such an increase has also been a source of finance for the universities, especially with full cost fees charged to students from outside Europe. In 1999 the government encouraged this marketing, setting a target of 25 per cent of the global market. This has led to great competition for recruitment of international students. Practice here has been variable, with some universities promising a great deal of support and offering little once the student has arrived. For the most part, however, universities have responded to the increase in students with great care, many appointing international student advisors.

Many academics have seen all this as 'treasury-led'. One estimate of the cost to a university of losing an international student is £60,000. Some departments rely on them for their research. At the same time, international students have brought new cultural perspectives to UK academia, universities have shown real care for them, and massive opportunities have been made available for a much wider international group. To facilitate these opportunities the government introduced a series of measures, including:

- Streamlining the visa process for students.
- Making it easier for international students to obtain permission to work in Britain.
- Increasing scholarships Some groups, often in partnership with each other also provided scholarships, including universities themselves, industry and non-governmental organizations.

This chapter will first examine the experience of the international student and begin to look at the whole phenomenon of culture shock and some of the expectations that international students bring with them. It will then look at pastoral responses, including pastoral counselling, community and network care, and care in the curriculum.

Culture Shock

Mary arrived in Plumpton at 1 p.m. after a journey of more than 16 hours. She caught a taxi from the station and asked to be taken to the university. She assumed that when she got there all would be obvious and that soon she would have a bed and be told what she would have to do. She didn't expect the driver to ask whereabout in the campus she wanted to go; she didn't know. Dropped at the front gate, with all her luggage, she had no idea what to do. She was exhausted and felt that she had left most of herself back in Nairobi. She had almost been late for the flight, partly because she had been dealing with the aftermath of her mother's funeral, and she simply hadn't had the chance to gather all her university papers and read them. In any case faced with the confusing mass of buildings none of this was what she could have expected. She might have asked someone, but one of the few thoughts that kept coming back to her were the words of her sister, who had been abroad, 'Never ask anything of your teachers, the British are very cold and prickly, they never have time for you, so it's not good to look as if you don't know anything.' Mary wandered around campus for two hours before finding the accommodation office. She eventually asked someone she felt wasn't a teacher. At the office she was told to wait, they were busy and she was two days late. Eventually she was told where she had to stay and with no assistance got to her flat, about half a mile away. There were other international students there who asked her where her bedding was. The bedding could only be obtained from the accommodation office and cost money. Reluctant to go back to the office she spent the first six nights without blanket or sheets, and only went back when she began to feel the effects of the cold. She did not sleep fully for the first fortnight.

It took Mary more than two months to settle in to her course, with great help from fellow international students. During that time she suffered poor concentration, sleepless nights, frequent nausea and irritability. She only shared her story, eventually, with a chaplain, on the second occasion he called at the flat.

Even Mary's arrival showed the beginning of what Oberg (1960) terms *culture shock*. This involves:

- Strain, caused by the physical and psychological effort of adapting to a new culture.
- Feelings of loss and deprivation with regard to family, friends, and even status, profession and possessions.
- A sense of being rejected by members of the new culture.
- Confusion about role, role expectation, and values. With this comes a questioning of identity and personal value.
- Surprise about new cultural demands and sometimes a sense of disgust or anger about the cultural differences.
- A sense of impotence because of the inability to cope with the new environment.

The vast majority of international students experience this and some writers suggest that it is an inevitable adaptive process. Other writers refer to culture fatigue, role shock, or pervasive ambiguity. As Bock (1970) notes, customary experiences and behaviour no longer have significant meaning, hence it is hard to understand or respond to another's behaviour. Culture shock heightens the feeling of being a stranger, of being different from everyone else. For many the key search is to try to understand and respond to the new ethos, customs, values and life meaning. A good example of this is a group of international students in one healthcare studies school. Several months into the course they began to study the care of the dying. The tutor began by asking all those present about how they saw death. A number of the British students fed back their views in the seminar, but no response was made by any of the international students. At the end of the seminar the tutor asked one of them about this. He replied, 'We never talk about death in the college, or amongst our colleagues. Very quickly when we got here we realized that no one talks about death, it is feared by everyone.' These students had picked up the cultural message that talk of death was taboo. If they were to share their much more open and accepting view of death they believed that this would contravene cultural practice and thus offend. Two things are underlined in this case. First, international students have very sharp antennae. They are actively searching for clues and cues about cultural meaning and behaviour. Second, in this case, they had picked up not simply on the general culture of Britain in regard to death but especially on the

Stages in culture shock

Stages	Perceptions	Emotional ranges
Contact	Differences are intriguing perceptions are screened and selected	Excitement, stimulation, euphoric, playful
Disintegration	Differences create an impact, contrasted and cultural reality cannot be screened out	Confusion, disorientation, loss, apathy, isolation, loneliness, inadequacy
Reintegration	Differences are rejected	Anger, rage, nervousness, anxiety, frustration
Autonomy	Differences and similarities are legitimized.	Self assured, relaxed, warm. Empathic
Independence	Differences and similarities are valued and significant	Trust, humour, love, full range of previous emotions

subculture of the health services, where death is often seen as a failure of the medical team, rather than a part of life.

Oberg explored further effects of losing 'the familiar signs and symbols of social intercourse' (Oberg 1960, 176). These include:

- Feelings of powerlessness, meaninglessness and *anomie*.
- Confusion. This can lead to an absent-minded 'far-away' stare, occasionally known as the tropical stare.
- Desire for dependence upon key figures.

Behaviour	Interpretations
Curiosity, interest, assured, impressionistic	Individual insulated by his/her culture. Differences as well as similarities provide rationalization for continuing, confirmation of status, role and identity.
Depression, withdrawal	Cultural differences begin to intrude. Growing awareness of being different leads to loss of self-esteem. Individual experiences loss of cultural support ties and misreads new cultural cues.
Rebellion, suspicion, rejection, hostility, exclusive, opinionated	Rejection of second culture causes preoccupation with dislikes; differences are projected. Negative behaviour, however, is a form of assertion and self-esteem.
Assured, controlled, independent, 'old hand', confident	Individual socially and linguistically capable of negotiating most new and different situations: he/she is assured of ability to survive new experiences.
Expressive, creative actualizing	Social, psychological and cultural differences accepted and enjoyed. Individual capable of exercising choice and responsibility, and able to create meaning for situations.

- Fits of anger over delays and minor frustrations. Sometimes the anger and confusion can lead to delays in learning the language of the host country or outright refusal to take classes.
- Fear of being robbed or cheated. For some this can verge on paranoia.
- Major anxiety about minor ailments.
- Immense desire to find someone of one's own nationality.
- Concern about physical factors such as food and drink, bedding and even dishes.
- For some there is a great concern for order.
- A continual low-level anxiety accompanied by depression.

Mary experienced many of these elements during her first week, an
experience that was exacerbated by the fact that the university in
question had at that time nothing in place to care for international
students who arrived late. It was also exacerbated by her own experience of bereavement. Mary also experienced a deep sense of homesickness. Homesickness is very much a part of many students'
experience but for the international student it can be profound and
sometimes debilitating (Fisher and Hood 1987).

Culture shock can be seen more in terms of stages or even of a life
cycle that extends over the period from the international student
being at university to their return home.

The stages of culture shock are neatly summed up by UKCOSA
(2003) in the table on pages 146–7.

As with all stage approaches, this must not be taken as invariant
and sequential. Many of these feelings might occur at once or be
returned to later. Viewed more in terms of a 'life cycle' approach it is
possible to see an initial honeymoon period which is part of the
initial contact. This then moves through the stages to independence
that can often be between three and six months into the course. For
those who are there for only a year, this can easily move into a second
cycle as the student begins to prepare for home. Initially this will
involve its own honeymoon stage filled by thoughts of home. This is
followed by the same stages as the first cycle, this time fuelled by
anxiety about how significant others at home might feel after this
time, by exam or dissertation anxiety, something made worse by fear
that obligations to family and to funding bodies at home might not
be met. This cycle is typically not as deep or prolonged as the first.

Culture shock can be prolonged when there is little social support,
and when the cultural, moral and spiritual conflicts experienced by
the student are too great. Many Muslim students find difficulty with
the mores of Western society. One female student gave the following testimony,

> I have had to accept many things I do not approve of and it is such
> a shock to me because of my own customs. It is as though every-
> thing I have been taught at home and all my different values do
> not count for anything here and I must become a different person
> to cope with it all. I think if my family could see me now they
> would think I have changed very much, to accept such things that
> are completely against my upbringing (Harris 1997, 39).

For many African Christians there is the difficult value clash to do with homosexuality. One African bishop doing a postgraduate degree was asked by staff and students to share his views. At all points he refused to be drawn. He knew that the values clash was such that it might offend his hosts. In this sense, the values of acceptance and harmony outweigh any particular controversies for the international student, and it is dealt with by bracketing the value conflict. Others, such as Mary, find that more difficult to do. She was someone with a very firm but fragile and limited belief system – that of a strongly literalist Christian. This made her feel increasingly guilty when she began to be tested and unsure when faced by the strongly postmodern culture of the UK. She also felt intense guilt at leaving her family behind.

Pastoral and Spiritual Care

The pastoral care response can be broadly divided into pastoral care and counselling, community care, and care in the curriculum.

Pastoral Care and Counselling

Kim, a first year Chinese student, came to see the chaplain at the end of the second semester. She was attractive and well turned out, and smiled pleasantly throughout the conversation. At first it was not clear why she had come. It later emerged that her department had informed her that she was being 'thrown out'. She explained that she had not attended many of the seminars or met work deadlines. She revealed that she was distressed, largely because her parents were in Britain, doing postgraduate work. She felt she was expected to follow them into this research. Beneath the smart exterior Kim was very depressed and had probably been so for some time. The chaplain advised her to go immediately to the campus medical practice and to relay her story. Her depression was confirmed and she returned to the department, which was able to negotiate a restart for the next academic year. Her personal tutor commented, 'We couldn't believe when the medics said she was depressed, she always seemed to be having a good time. We assumed that there was nothing wrong with her and she just wasn't trying.'

Johnny and Mark, two students from Hong Kong came to the chaplain with the belief that their flatmate, Luke, was possessed by a demon. They described how their friend exhibited animalistic behaviour. He would bray and howl, froth at the mouth and claw at the walls. The chaplain listened carefully, enabling them to say how they felt and what they felt needed to happen. It emerged that at the heart of the problem was not so much the fear of possession as the annoyance at their flatmate because he was affecting their work. They wanted all this behaviour to stop or they were going to leave. The chaplain spoke about the Western view of possession and how this was not dismissed but that it always had to be checked out in an empirical way. They accepted this and agreed that they would encourage their flat mate to bring his problem to the chaplain. In the end the chaplain visited the student in question. It emerged that he had felt possessed before coming to Britain. A member of a charismatic church there, he had suffered rejection by his girlfriend and was praying, 'manifesting himself' to God, when he felt that something had entered him. The chaplain enabled him to speak about how he felt, especially about his faith, about the rejection by his girlfriend, and about the times of possession. As he worked through those feelings, the possession symptoms began to disappear. After three sessions they shared a time of prayer and a ritual of new beginnings.

Many international students find the idea of counselling very difficult. Western counselling is reactive, person-centred and developmental. In the first of these, the student has to come to the counsellor and have some indication of the problem that needs attention. Kim had spent a whole year precisely avoiding such contact, hiding her depression from all significant people, including her parents. She finally came for help only when she was about to be ejected from the university. For her, depression, and visits to counsellors, were associated with failure. It was a matter of shame to give in to the symptoms of anxiety, loss of concentration and so on. This was partly about the need to maintain 'face'. It is also about not having any cultural means or vocabulary of expressing distress, other than in very formal or ritualistic ways. The result for many international students is that they are unable to understand or accept the strong feelings that may be emerging in them.

This was very much the case for Luke. He had a mixture of real grief at the loss of his girlfriend, perfectionist shame because of the difficulties that he was finding in his course, and a strong sense of the need to express all his feelings in terms of the Christian culture that he learned. Hence, the inner turmoil was expressed in almost ritualistic possession language. When he explored the feelings surrounding his 'possession' he noted a sense of confusion, isolation, fear, loss of control. Once each of these was worked through he was able to take responsibility for articulating those feelings and from there to restart his relationship with his church from a different basis. None of this is to deny the possibility of possession. It is to say that in working with international students it is important to begin with a pastoral care approach which is person-centred, focusing on the feelings which underlie the particular cultural expression.

This was also important in response to the two flatmates who came. The expectation for them was not to come to a person-centred counsellor but rather to an expert who could respect their situation and do something about their problem. It was important therefore not to dismiss the different culture, but to listen and respect the strong sense of the supernatural. The pastoral process can be summarized as follows:

- Enable the person to articulate the story. Kim at no point had been given permission to do this. The department was the last place she could feel comfortable in doing so. Departmental practice in such situations might best look to enabling international students who are not achieving targets to speak with either chaplains or the Student Union.
- Enable the spiritual and cultural elements of that story to be set out. In this case it was the acceptance of the possibility of possession. It is important therefore not to move in with a critique of the supernatural or to get across any sense of this being questioned.
- Enable the student to articulate how he feels about the experience which he has described. This is a very important element in response to the international student. There is a parallel approach in terms of pastoral care for mental health. As Swinton notes, psychotherapy which enables the spiritual element of therapy to be drawn out needs to pay genuine attention to the feeling underlying even the most bizarre expression of paranoia, enabling the patient to feel understood (Swinton 2001).
- The process then moves into a cultural dialogue (Lartey 1997). As

noted above, for many international students, there is a strong desire to find out how the home culture views any particular thing. In this case, it was important for the two flatmates to hear alongside their cultural perspective what Western culture had to offer. Simply to buy into their culture and set upon exorcism would not have been true to this aspect of the process. On the contrary they were keen to hear the alternative approaches, especially the scientific approaches, which they could respect from their science background. Hence, what was emerging was perception of the underlying feelings and what the person wanted, and alongside this several different cultural perspectives of the experience in question. Each was respected, and the students could see how it was possible to hold them together and not need to judge one above others.

None of the students who came to the chaplaincy with a problem saw this in terms of looking for self-development. On the contrary, they saw the problem in terms of searching for a framework that would enable them to cope, and live up their different 'life-scripts', sets of expectations. However, pastoral counselling offered by the chaplain did enable further personal exploration. The reflection enabled their life meaning to be articulated and different life meanings to be brought to the person's consciousness. As Halmos (1961) noted, any contradictions that may emerge at this point are then down to the person to take responsibility for. The tensions for the two friends were resolved fairly quickly. In the end, the perfectionist script, in terms of work, was the one that they wanted to pursue and the possession script was simply another way of looking at a disturbing problem. For Luke there were major questions raised about a very conditional and perfectionist faith, and he resolved to work through that further.

In all this, there is a dynamic that moves the student through to a genuinely dialogic approach, away from simply seeing the chaplain as expert and into a negotiated solution with the student taking responsibility for meaning. Just as the chaplain is not an 'expert' it is important to remember that he might also be prey to prejudices not previously noticed. Tuckwell (2003) notes the importance of monitoring these, especially though pastoral supervision.

Finance

Some international students come with expectations that the Church will help them in any financial difficulties. Where there is little chance of support, it may be important to encourage a speedy return home. For many who are in financial difficulties, however, the urge to get the degree overrides any financial constraints. The chaplain can make use of the different networks on and off campus to effect support. In one case this led to an ordained Anglican postgraduate linking into the local diocese, being given a house for occasional work, and being used in services in the deanery. There might also be grant bodies in the local area. In general the Student Union and international student office are important resources for exploring possible areas of finance. For up to date information on financial matters and other advice see 'Student Advice' on the UKCOSA website or contact the Churches Commission for International Students (see page 162 for details).

Cults

At the initial stages of culture shock any international student can be vulnerable to cults. Inevitably they lack of any criteria with which to judge particular religious groups, especially when the impression is given of a formal church. A response to cults is detailed in Chapter 9.

Community and Network Care

The vast majority of international students do not go for individual care or counselling and it is community support that enables smooth transition through culture shock. This is at the heart of any theology of pastoral care with the theme of caring for the stranger in the midst. Bochner, McLeod and Lin (1977) suggest a threefold friendship pattern for international students that will begin to fulfil major needs:

- *Primary, monocultural networks.* These are made up of close friends and especially other 'sojourning compatriots'. The key function of such national groups is to provide a safe environment of support in which cultural value and life meaning can be articulated and affirmed.

- *Secondary, bicultural networks.* This is the key relationship between the student and academics and support staff, on and off campus, who enable academic success. As shall be seen below, this is a much more important area for international students than for indigenous students.
- *Tertiary, multicultural networks.* These consist of friends and acquaintances who provide friendship, non-task-oriented activities and a wider entry into the culture of the host nation.

The importance of any of these groups will vary according to the student and according to several variables, including site of accommodation, previous experience abroad and so on. However, whenever an international student comes to the chaplaincy it is important to ascertain just what support groups he or she is in and to be able to refer him to appropriate ones. The chaplaincy team, therefore, has to have a grasp of the different networks and possibilities. For some students there may be no monocultural groups, and the functions of such a group may have to be worked on in another context.

The Church and chaplaincy falls into the third of these groups, but may take on the function of any of the others, as shall be seen below. It is critical to ensure that communities are maintained through the whole year, not just in semesters.

The Practice of Community

There are many ways in which community can be practised for international students, including:

- Having hosts at the train station or airport to help the person find their way and to deal with their basic physical needs, guiding them through the system. Chaplaincy and all Christian student groups can be involved in this process.
- The development of an international student club. Such a club is best 'manned' by volunteers from the local churches and student groups. This can give a good ratio of helpers to students, enabling real attention to need, and link the student into further networks via the local churches. The club can function systematically, enabling students to articulate their cultural identity through evenings of shared cultural beliefs or different national foods and so on, and enabling them to explore the local culture. The latter

can be done through local visits, presentations and so on. International student clubs can also lead to subgroups such as Bible study. While the aim is not to evangelize per se, many international students, especially from Asia, show a great thirst for learning about the culture, central to which are the religious beliefs and rituals. Local church volunteers can also set up English language classes. The advantage of these classes, often run by retired church members, is that they can be flexible and tied into the often busy student's timetable.

- Induction events. The hectic world of induction can be difficult for the international student. Welcome can function in two ways. First, it can give the basis for future support, linking in to the different student groups. Second, it can provide supportive and friendly ways to enable groups of students to articulate and recognize the process of culture shock that they are going through. One example of this, which has been successful, is a brief play put on by chaplains and experienced international students which takes them though the different stages in a humorous way. Another approach is to set up debriefing sessions over dinner. These can be held three or four weeks into the semester, the objective being to enable the people to talk together about their experience, and look forward. The idea of debriefing in this context is very positive. It sounds very practical and carries with it no overtones of crisis or failure.
- Continued support. The international students club and the local church networks can themselves begin to respond to needs of the students both by providing material resources for students in need, and also providing family hospitality on a regular basis, but especially in vacation times.
- The chaplaincy can work with several different groups on and off campus to coordinate events involving international students, such as One World Week celebrations.

Care in the Church

Most Christian international students are concerned to find a local worshipping community that can be their base for their time away from home. Chaplaincy should develop networks with the local churches that can ensure warm experienced host communities. An annual meeting with the local churches can raise the issue of training and how the chaplaincy can support the churches in their ministry. Local churches can combine to offer volunteers for all the projects noted above or for making available material resources for those in need. Some churches have provided practical support such as crèches for international student families. Others have stopped giving money on a regular basis to overseas aid, instead choosing to support a scholarship, sometimes in association with university departments. The aim of this is to make a long-term difference, enabling qualifications and education that can be used in areas of need.

International students can, of course, be a terrific resource, bringing insights from their churches which can enrich local congregations and networks, including racial justice groups. Providing space for the student in worship and meetings enables the student to articulate his narrative, affirm his identity and be genuinely appreciated by a supportive group. The new student's perspective can enable links with his home church, building up the story so that the local church becomes a part of it. The church then can be the focus of many different networks, including local schools. Worship also provides a context for ritual celebration, and sharing of worship styles, which once more affirms identity. The importance of ritual at all levels of care for the international student cannot be overestimated. At key times of crisis, ritual can provide a strong focus. Bereaved international students can often not get back for the funeral, or to fulfil their family duties. Chaplaincy can provide memorial services which help focus on all these areas.

Such support can of course involve the student's family if they are there, perhaps in collaboration with the chaplaincy and the university international student advisor.

The church can move into other enriching links with international students and student groups, involving them in their one World Week celebrations, using international student musicians and choirs in worship, or offering rehearsal space.

Finally, church members can offer hospitality to international students during Christmas and other vacations. This can be co-ordinated locally by the chaplaincy or worked through the different host schemes, run locally or nationally, and often co-ordinated by the international student office.

Care in the Curriculum

As noted above, the bicultural network is important to the international student. The academic element of this is very important, for several reasons:

- The international student often arrives burdened by family expectations.
- He may be supported by funding organizations which have a major interest in his academic success.
- Academic success may be tied very immediately to a job that he will return to.

For many students, especially postgraduates, this contributes to real stress. There are also different academic, communication and learning cultures which can compound this stress.

Academic Cultures

Cortazzi and Jin (1997) note that the Western academic culture tends to emphasize:

- Individual orientation, which stresses independence of mind.
- Creativity and originality.
- Peer group relationships in the discussion of knowledge, leading to discussion, argument and mutual challenge between peers and academic staff.
- Active involvement in all aspects of learning.
- Verbal explicitness.
- Awareness of alternatives and their critical evaluation.

They note that in international student groups, and especially among the Chinese, a very different academic culture emerges, involving:

- A sense of collective consciousness.
- Stress on hierarchical relationships.
- Passive involvement in the educational process.
- Dependence on authority.
- Stress on mastery and transmission of data.

- The importance of agreement, harmony and maintaining 'face'. 'Face' is neatly summed up by Yua-fai Ho (1976, 883) as 'the respectability or deference which a person can claim for himself from others, by virtue of the position he occupies in his social network and the degree to which he is judged to have functioned adequately in that position'.
- Stress on single solution.
- The assumption that the proper solution should be accepted.

One illustration of these differences is cited by Cortazzi and Jin (1997, 84). A Saudi Arabian student asked his tutor which research method was best. He was told that all the approaches outlined had their advantages and disadvantages, and that the answer to the question depended upon the particular research context. Detailed examples were given. The response was, 'Which method does the staff use here?' The tutor repeated the answer and concluded that the staff used a full range of methods. The final response was, 'Which method do you use?' The student later admitted that he pre-supposed that there was a best method to finding a single solution, which stemmed ultimately from one (religious) truth.

Communication cultures

Several modes of communication may give very different signals to tutors or to support persons. Middle Eastern students can easily be seen as overbearing and aggressive if they use the heavy intonation, relatively loud voices and rhetorical exaggeration which may be part of home culture. One student produced a perfect PhD viva until the very last question, which led him to respond in the rhetorical mode and almost led to disaster.

The use of pauses in conversation can also give rise to problems. Different cultures have different valuation of pauses. Equally the pause might involve real underlying difficulties. Jin reports one postgraduate interview in which the Chinese student gave several long pauses. The tutor was perplexed by this and found it hard to respond, being unsure whether the student had understood his initial comments (Jin 1992). Parallel to the tutor's difficulty was the dilemma suffered by the student. If the student was to say that he did not understand, this would count as failure on his part and lead to loss of face. Moreover, by implication, if he had raised this he would have been critical of the tutor's skills, thereby causing him to lose face.

Other differences in communication include styles of presentation. Chinese students, for instance, in speaking and writing, will tend to take a long time to establish common ground and prepare an argument before getting to the main point (Young 1994; Scollon and Scollon 1995, 81). In contrast, British tutors look for a clear indication of the main point of the argument early on.

Such problems with communication might also disguise an underlying difference in the culture of learning.

The Culture of Learning

Several cultures, especially the Chinese, see the process of learning as teacher-centred (Cortazzi and Jin 1997). The teacher should be an authority on his subject but also a model in terms of behaviour. They will teach the student not only about the subject but about life. For some this means the teacher becomes a parent figure. In the light of that the student owes the teacher respect, and should listen carefully and reflect to himself, developing skills as an apprentice might. This kind of cultural expectation often leads international postgraduate students to look for a very deep relationship with their supervisor, one which will see the student frequently calling on the supervisor. The very different view of many supervisors is that postgraduates should work independently and visit them infrequently. This looks to the view of the teacher as an enabler and a friendly critic, and of the student as someone who should declare ignorance in order to learn.

Four things should be stressed in relation to these cultural differences:

- Awareness of these differences provides a useful framework for communication. However, it should not be assumed they will apply in all situations. Some students actively want to alter their cultural approaches. Others find them very deeply rooted and this can lead to anxiety and depression, particularly in postgraduates who feel that they cannot relate to their supervisors.
- Awareness of these cultural differences can help the chaplain to act as broker between teacher and student if there is a breakdown. Alternatively the chaplain can help the student to develop strategies to work with the teacher.

- Similar differences may operate in other areas of the student's life.
- Good practice in relation to these issues includes:
  - Reflection on what cultural styles are being used.
  - In particular being aware of the different ways of showing respect, how the student takes his turn to speak, how he responds to critical evaluation, what part pauses play in the conversation and so on.
  - Where possible, the student should be given the chance to speak about what he expects of the learning experience, and how he sees the teacher and student roles.
  - Where possible, there should be the development of a learning contract which establishes what teacher and student are happy with in terms of practice.

Conclusions

The aims of chaplaincy to international students might include:

- Coordinating the International Student Club or alternative chaplaincy hospitality.
- Linking with the local churches, perhaps through a group of staff and students.
- Linking into the existing networks on campus. In addition to the links to international student advisors and pastoral support networks this may mean working with the equal opportunities office. Many such offices have a creative brief which takes in the rights of the international student. In one case this led to chaplaincy and the equal opportunities office developing a One World Week celebration. This can also extend network care to more than one university. In one city a chaplain chairs the international student liaison group, which consists of key workers from both the major universities and some from the community. It enables effective and creative support across the board. It is also a strong platform for prophetic work, looking to strengthen the care of the stranger in HE and FE.
- The chaplaincy can also ensure that there is effective contact with the major ethnic student groups.
- There should also be training for the team. This can involve either linking into the university professional development services, or

bringing trainers from UKCOSA. However this is done, it is useful to have the UKCOSA training manual and handbook, which includes excellent material on developing cultural awareness.

To ensure that all this is maintained, the chaplaincy team might appoint one chaplain, full- or part-time, to coordinate this area.

References

Bochner, S., McLeod, B. and Lin, A., ' Friendship patterns of overseas students: a functional model', *International Journal of Psychology* 12, 1977, pp. 277–99.

Bock, P., *Culture Shock: A Reader in Modern Psychology*, Knopf, New York, 1970.

Cortazzi, M. and Jin, L., 'Communication for learning across cultures', in McNamara, D. and Harris, R., *Overseas Students in Higher Education*, Routledge, London, 1997, pp. 76–90.

Fisher, S. and Hood, B., 'The stress of transition to university', *British Journal of Psychology* 78, 1987, pp. 425–41.

Halmos, P., *Faith of the Counsellor*, Constable, London, 1961.

Harris, R., 'Overseas students in the UK system', in McNamara, D. and Harris, R., *Overseas Students in Higher Education*, Routledge, London, 1997, pp. 30–45.

Jin, L., '*Academic cultural expectations and second language use*', unpublished PhD, University of Leicester, 1992.

Lago, C. and Humphrys, N., 'Issues of difference in further and higher education', in Lees, J. and Vaspe, A. (eds), *Clinical Counselling in Further and Higher Education*, Routledge, London, 1999.

Lartey, E., *In Living Colour*, Cassell, London, 1997.

Oberg, J., 'Culture Shock: adjustment to new cultural environments', *Practical Anthropology* 7, 1960, pp. 177–82.

Robinson, S. and Benwell, M., 'Christian Chaplaincy in the Postmodern University', *Modern Believing*, 41(1), 1999.

Scollon, R. and Scollon, S., *Intercultural Communication*, Blackwell, Oxford, 1995.

Swinton, J., *Spirituality and Mental Health Care*, Jessica Kingsley, London, 2001.

Tuckwell, G., 'White therapists and racial awareness', *Counselling and Psychotherapy Journal*, 14(2), 2003, pp. 12–16.

UKCOSA Manual, UKCOSA, London, 2003.

Young, L., *Crosstalk and Culture in Sino-American Communication*, Cambridge University Press, Cambridge, 1994.

Yua-fai Ho, D., 'On the Concept of Face', *American Journal of Sociology* 81, 1976, pp. 867–84.

Contacts

Churches Commission for International Students (CCIS): ccis@ctbi.org.uk
UKCOSA: The Council for International Education: www.ukcosa.org.uk

Part 4

Prophetic Work

9

Prophecy

I have already noted that in an organization with so many different narratives there will inevitably be many different value conflicts. It is understandable then that chaplains in all sectors see the role of prophet as central to their practice.

The prophet is traditionally seen as one who, in Pattison's words, 'forthtells the action of God to a community in the present events of history' (Pattison 1993, 177). This is primarily about standing out for justice, and thus demands moral, social and political awareness and response. In the context of Higher Education, prophecy may involve several different areas:

- *Whistleblowing.* This involves reporting previously unrevealed unethical issues to a higher authority. These may be of a financial, sexual, drug related nature, involving staff or students. It is highly unlikely that the chaplain will be in a position to blow any whistles. If he does get to know about such problems it will tend to be through pastoral care and would therefore be constrained by confidentiality. Nonetheless, the chaplain may well be in a position to support and counsel whistleblowers, and it is possible that she may be faced by the challenge to blow the whistle on some behaviours.

- *Issues of university need.* This is about standing out for significant need within the university. An example of this would be where the institution lacks an important support service for students or staff. One chaplaincy, for instance, spent several years helping to develop counselling services and the effective co-ordination of the student support services as a whole in a university community that was not totally convinced of the need. Another example might be standing up for the value of community in the prevailing consumer culture.

- *Broader issues of justice.* This is where the practice of the university or some part of the university comes up against matters of justice in the wider world, such as:
  - The physics professor who accepts research funding from defence budgets.
  - The department that makes links with problem multinational companies.
  - The university that offers an honorary degree to a right-wing American Secretary of State, or makes strong links with an oppressive regime, because this will lead to an increase in international students.
  - The university that consistently ignores the problems created by students in the local community.
  - The leisure outlet in the university that encourages students to increase alcohol consumption.
- *Issues of national concern*, such as student debt, or the government's policies on Higher Education.
- *Issues of equity.* This moves into the area of rights. It may involve, for instance, other faiths. Are there, for instance, proper facilities in the university for Muslim worship, or which take into account the different faith festivals during exam times?
- *Issues of integrity.* In terms of university practice, for instance, is the university recruitment of international students ethical? Does it give a realistic picture to the would-be students, and does it provide the support and provisions which it promises? Does it have a code of practice for this?
- *Issues of global concern.* Does the university take seriously issues such as Third World debt and the environment?

The dynamic of prophecy here seeks to explore the moral obligations and responsibility that a university might have in these areas. All such issues are a reasonable area of concern for the chaplain.

Contrasting with such prophecy is *advocacy*. This can be defined as representing the particular needs and concerns of a student or group of students. It is not a matter of fighting for the rights of the student so much as being with them and ensuring proper support at times of need, whatever the rights and wrongs of the student in that situation. This will be examined more closely towards the end of this chapter.

The prophetic stance is often seen as that of an individual, best fulfilled by someone who is external to the organization, and is context specific, with a 'word' for a particular situation (Gill 1981). This can lead to adversarial relations, exemplified by Amos, whose words were too hard to bear (Amos 7.10). Such a model of prophecy is difficult to use in chaplaincy. If the Johannine theology is respected then the chaplain has to be seen as part of the organization. He may not be 'owned' by that organization, but he is certainly not outside it. Nonetheless, the chaplain's position gives her real prophetic perspective. Longbottom, in the context of the healthcare chaplaincy, notes that the chaplain is the only member of the team who is not part of the hierarchy and thus is ideally suited to the role of asking questions of the institution about their practice (Longbottom 1987, 89). Grainger (1979) picks up the Johannine theology, suggesting that the chaplain can be seen in the role of the jester or fool. The fool in *King Lear*, for instance, is someone who is precisely in the court, indeed close to the king, but not of it, not part of the hierarchy. Precisely because of this, he is able to challenge the king in a most direct way. Two questions immediately arise from this.

1 Who might the prophet be in any situation?
2 What is the nature and practice of prophecy in HE?

This chapter examines these questions under the heads of covenant and contract, conversation and collaboration.

Contract and Covenant

As noted in Chapter 4, prophetic work is part of the chaplaincy covenant. The capacity to enable the institution to face the truth of what it might be doing is primary.

It is important to make clear the prophetic role as part of any contract. This is especially the case if the chaplain is employed by the institution. The principal of one Scottish university insisted at one point that a key importance of the chaplain was that she should honestly reflect back to him what she saw in terms of intelligence (i.e. data) and values. Lamdin (1999), writing about chaplaincy in general, notes three things that are necessary for the chaplain to begin to make a prophetic contribution:

- A high level of trust, such that the institution can be confident that it will not be attacked by the chaplain.

- Good knowledge of the institution from the inside, its organization, business and politics.
- Great care about how any prophecy is communicated.

Assurances of this nature can be part of any contract, such that the chaplain's independence of thought and particular reflection is acknowledged and valued. This also applies to chaplains paid by the university.

Conversation

Conversation sounds too cosy by half. It sounds like a gentleman's agreement to be 'civilized' about the whole thing. In fact this is very far from the case. Prophecy in this context is essentially about enabling reflection and transparency that allows any practice to be brought to light and dealt with appropriately. There are three possible stages to this prophecy:

- *Establish data*. This may involve knowledge from many different people. Where there is a questionable practice then it should be verified. This may mean keeping or encouraging others to keep good records. It may also mean consulting with experts in this area to confirm the significance of the data. Any data can also be checked out with the chaplain's senior in the Church. The senior can help the chaplain reflect on the options and what motives there might be for acting. In particular the temptation to be cast as heroic saviour or to fight single-handed battles can be tested out. Whatever the situation, it is important that the senior knows of this, not least because if the issue becomes public then he or she will doubtless be brought into the debate.
- *Values*. A careful analysis of all involved in the issue and of the underlying values should take place. Once again, this would benefit from discussion with a senior. As shall be seen below there may be value conflicts, with very different views of what is acceptable. There may be a value conflict within the organization, with, for example, a university statement setting out one view of research or social responsibility, which already forms the basis for making a judgement on the issue in question. Conversational communication will enable non-judgemental critique and be able to highlight such value conflicts.

- *Prophetic action.* The next step is to bring the issue before the person who is directly concerned. This may range from the vice-chancellor to student groups. In the conversational context this then allows the value conflict to come to the surface. The initial aim then is to encourage the person in question to respond to the value conflict and seek to do something about it. If this is a matter of whistleblowing, then the organization's methods for dealing with this should be investigated. It may be appropriate simply to refer this to a particular committee, or to the supervisor. If it is a decision taken by the executive, then it may be appropriate to refer it to one of the major boards, senate or council. All such due process should be gone through so that all involved are respected and, through the medium of reflective dialogue, are challenged to examine the issues and respond. It may be at the end of all this that the issues have not been worked through and there still exists a glaring inequity or an action that needs to be questioned. In which case a more public stance can be taken, providing that the university is kept informed of how this will be achieved and that it is done with respect, avoiding any adversarial dynamic. For the most part, university administrators and executives are very aware of the potential for problems when it comes to value conflicts. Hence, they actively value early discussions about the issues involved and what can be done. This means being involved in the processes in the university which reflect on decision-making, especially committee work.

  What is less than effective is to move into an aggressive prophetic dynamic. Such a dynamic runs the risk of being individualistic, and thus of not being aware of the whole picture. It can also lead to polarization and demonization (Robinson 1994).

Hence, it is important to examine motives. For the most part, universities will respect a prophetic stance which goes beyond such dialogue. One chaplaincy, for instance, publicly stood by the Association of University Teachers (AUT) when it was in dispute with the management. The chaplaincy centre was at the front gate of the university and provided food, coffee and shelter for the freezing pickets from 6.30 a.m. In another case, the chaplaincy organized a public meeting to give space to a whistleblower on campus. The management was warned about the event and fully accepted it and the way in which it was handled. Another chaplaincy organized a series of public debates in collaboration with departments to question university policy on investments. The key to successful prophecy in both cases was to make it issue, not group or personality, centred.

Whichever route is taken, prophecy is most effective when collaborative.

Collaborative Prophecy

The role of prophecy can easily be seen as exclusive and individualistic when in fact there are many in any university who are prophets, and precisely 'in the world but not of it'. Good examples of this are student medical practices, the student union and staff unions. Student medical practices tend to be either independent from the university or to work through a services level agreement. Student unions can only function if, like staff unions, they are seen as independent from the university. At the same time they offer so many important services, not least in terms of welfare advice and support, that they are seen by universities as essential to staff and student care. On the whole the university values such independent perspectives.

The chaplaincy can work together with such groups around particular issues. There are at least four ways, for instance, in which chaplaincy can work prophetically with the student union.

First, they can work on specific campaigns, including drugs and alcohol, mental health, safe sex, and students and debt. These are aimed at changing behaviour, either of individual students or of organizations, and affecting cultures. This recognizes that while prophecy from the union majors on autonomy and tolerance, it also attempts to influence choice in practice. This involves raising awareness and encouraging personal responsibility.

A second level of working with the student union is in broader campaigns such as Fairtrade. This can include joint debates, encouraging the sale of Fairtrade goods in the union shops and setting up temporary Fairtrade stalls in the union foyer.

Third, things become even more interesting when values begin to conflict. This is the critical experience of having two prophetic groups on campus who advocate very different things. A good example is abortion. One union ran a campaign on abortion looking at it in terms of freedom of choice. It stood out against the pro-life position, seeing it as taking away from the procreative choice of women. This also involved several thousand pounds from the union budget to support any student who wished to have an abortion. The response from the chaplaincy was to organize three debates over a week which brought together students from very different positions. The result was a challenge on the union position, showing that even according to its own values of tolerance and liberalism it was being partial. They agreed to provide support of equal amount for any student who wanted to keep her baby.

A fourth area of work with the student union can take the chaplaincy into even greater complexity as the following case illustrates.

> A small conservative Christian student group was temporarily banned from the Student Union because they had been preaching aggressively in the foyer of the Union building, in particular against homosexuals. The Union was now looking to bring this before their disciplinary committee and effect a permanent ban. The Christian Union, as a society of the Student Union, was very concerned about this. This president wanted to support the group in question. He felt that if they were banned then the CU should also withdraw from the Student Union. He was concerned to show support for another evangelical organization, and to show solidarity in terms of the stance on homosexuality.

In this case prophecy takes on a reflective and complex tone. In fact there were several different 'prophets':

- An extreme Christian group.
- An evangelical group.
- The executive of the evangelical group, with their own concerns.
- The chaplaincy, who had links to all the groups in question.
- The Christian Forum, who were concerned about homophobia.
- The student union, who were against homophobia and the generally aggressive tone of the preaching in the union building.
- The interfaith forum also had interesting views on this, not least because some members of one of the groups were against homosexuality.

This heady mixture of principles and politics looked about to explode, with competing prophets looking for the most effective public stance.

The issue came together in a meeting with the CU executive, one of the chaplains and the honorary advisors of the CU (local church leaders). The group carefully worked through the events of what had happened and how the student union had responded. They then reflected together on the different values which were there and how important they were:

- The student union stressed the value of freedom of speech, balanced by an aversion to any form of homophobia or intolerance.
- The small evangelical group believed in the inerrancy of Scripture and the need to communicate the gospel.
- The Christian Union argued for the importance of Scripture, and of the freedom to proclaim the gospel.

Each of these values was then tested and a variety of conflicts began to emerge. First, the president revealed the additional value of keeping solidarity with another evangelical group. Other members of the executive began to question this. They also argued that the student union values were very important and that in signing up to be a student union society they had agreed to abide by them. The president then argued that if they did not make a stand this might cause a split in the Christian Union. It was, he said, his responsibility as president to keep the show on the road. This in turn was questioned. Would the CU really split and, in any case, was it the job of the executive to simply keep the group together? As one member said, 'Isn't it rather our job to ensure that we keep the truth before the members and, in the light of that, God will keep us together?' Second, it became clear that the behaviour of the small evangelical group was in certain respects not acceptable. They were aggressive and offensive.

It was possible therefore for the CU both to affirm the small group in their biblical work but also to challenge them in the way they did it, and to suggest alternative ways of exploring these areas which would not offend.

The role of the chaplain in all this was to facilitate and to enable the different values to be heard and to enable a move away from dramatic prophecy that would have resulted in the marginalization of the CU to a much more productive prophecy.

In the end the prophetic stance was both to the fellow Christian groups and to the union. The union had at one point banned all public reading from the Bible. This event provided the opportunity to question that and to open up the union for genuine faith sharing, across the board. The final result was a series of meetings with other Christian groups to talk about the whole issue and how they all stood on the question of homosexuality. Differences were still there but greater openness enabled a development of trust. All the different parties were affirmed in their different prophetic stances and the complexity of the situation was respected, leading to a creative response and to renewed relationships. Dialogue in all this had led to critical conversation and mutual challenge.

Committee Work

An important area of collaborative prophecy, where issues can be addressed early, is committee work. Good committee work is always part of the reflective process for the whole of the university and its parts. This means that if the chaplain is part of that reflection he can put in a real contribution to the prophetic perspective. Some possibilities include:

- *Commercial and residential committees.* Such committees have pastoral and disciplinary concerns alongside finance. The chaplain can directly contribute, e.g. when it comes to ensuring that pastoral and discipline are brought together, or keeping the principle of community before the committee. This can result in the development of guidelines for hall wardens which take into account both. Equally he can look to the spiritual well-being of the students, looking, for instance, to the provision of quiet space. He is then at the sharp end of a learning organization.
- *The equality or equal opportunities office.* This is an area which is growing, taking into account all aspects of the university. Working with such an office can help to soften any aggressive target or rights approach and focus on community initiatives – such as a jointly organized One World Week.
- *Student support committees.* Chaplains might be simply part of these and contribute towards the strategic development of student services.
- *Ethics committees.* Chaplains can become involved in a variety of ethics committees, commenting on anything from research procedures to international student policy. In one university a chaplain was asked to draft a policy for international student recruitment.

Pastoral Care and Prophecy

Prophecy may also occur in a pastoral context. A professor of physics came to talk through a major ethical dilemma about funding. He knew that the department's financial future would be assured if he accepted a research grant from the Ministry of Defence that was related to major weapon systems. He was not a Christian but had come to the chaplain because of his reputation for taking such issues seriously and not polarizing the argument. The chaplain enabled him to reflect on the data, values and possibilities in the issue, focusing on how the professor saw his integrity. In consequence he chose to share the issue with his department. They chose not to accept the grant, and together identified other sources of income that dealt with the finance problems.

Whistleblowing

As noted above it is possible for the chaplain to support any whistleblower or on rare occasions to make some fact public himself. Whistleblowing, however, is best seen in terms of developing the university as a transparent learning organization such that:

- It has a proper committee structure which picks up matters of justice and ethical concern as part of any planning or decision-making process. Armstrong, Dixon and Robinson (1999) refer to this, in an engineering context, as an ethical audit.
- A policy for whistleblowing is in place (see Armstrong, Dixon and Robinson 1999, 57). Where it is not, then the chaplain, along with perhaps any Centre of Business and Professional Ethics on campus, might encourage its development.

External Networks of Prophecy

They can be on a local or national level. There is no doubt that there may be times when it is appropriate for prophecy to come from outside. This may involve church leaders, members of court, the alumni of the university and so on.

The University of Plumpton agrees to take funding from the local tobacco firm to establish a chair of business ethics. The university has taken quite some time to work through this process and argues that:

1 It consulted all relevant bodies, including those who deal with cancer research.
2 It followed all the proper processes in applying for funding.
3 No major industry in that area is free from the financial influence of tobacco.

Once the news is announced the university is hit with a maelstrom of bad publicity.

The first thing to say about this case is that the ethical reflection of the university was very narrow. The whole question of the social responsibility of a university was not examined. The second point is that with this high level public event there were many external prophets, from ASH to the cancer research organizations. In such a context it would be reasonable for church leaders to become involved, both through public comment and debate, direct communication with the vice-chancellor, and where the leader is on the university court by formally raising the issue there.

The role of the chaplain as being part of the ethical reflection on this case might be to co-ordinate some of the responses and to propose that a social responsibility code be drawn up.

In the area of international students, links can be built with national bodies such as UKCOSA.

Two-way Prophecy

We tend to assume that prophetic messages are aimed *at* the institution or its members. However, if chaplaincy is to encourage transparency on campus then it might also encourage such transparency in the Church. The chaplaincy is a good centre for enabling dialogue which invites others to share a prophetic word with us. Hence, for example where there is debate on homosexuality it is important to invite the gay and lesbian society of the union, and other such groups. It is amazing how much sharper the debate becomes when Christians have to listen respectfully to non-Christians. Chaplaincy also provides a safe place for local churches to be part of such debates.

Cults

An area where chaplains are quite often called upon to urge public action is in relation to so-called cults. Headlines such as 'Hell cult hits campus' set up a relationship with cults which sees them as entirely evil and out to prey on the vulnerable student body.

In fact cults or new religious movements (NRMs) are a very real problem for universities. Many NRMs will target students during intro-week, with the aim of recruiting. Their methods vary, including:

- Sitting next to single students in popular city centre coffee outlets.
- Infiltrating events in intro-week, such as intro-week cafés on campus.
- Infiltrating halls of residence through student members.
- Leafleting just off campus or outside the student union.

Problems with NRMs

NRMs cause problems for several different groups on campus.

- *University*. Their presence causes the local press and often parents to become anxious. However, while they might have difficulty with the methods and ideas of the NRM they are bound by their commitment to freedom of expression, and cannot easily exclude them from the campus or precinct.
- *The Christian evangelical groups*. Because the NRMs have a public profile and evangelize, they are often confused by others with groups like the CU. However, the CU has a strong sense of the difference in theology and practice.
- *Families*. A typical response from students who enter certain NRMs is increasingly to polarize relationships with their parents.
- *Students*. Students are the victims of these groups. However, they willingly enter into them, not least because they give the impression of being both established as a church but also different from the institutional churches. In this they stress their immense care for the student and build up a sense of dependency. This dynamic moves the student away from their family and encourages a black and white view of the world and issues. This is often accompanied by demands for both time and money.
- *International students*. International students are particularly

vulnerable, because they do not see the difference between such groups and evangelical churches and assume that they have some authority.

Students enter such groups out of their own volition and will leave only by the same route. The idea of rescue and deprogramming is morally very questionable. Hence, any prophecy is best in terms of helping the student to develop a healthy critical response to any group which wants to recruit them. Condemnation of any particular group is likely to have only the opposite effect, of hardening the attitude of both group and student. More effective are posters and leaflets (supplied by INFORM) which raise awareness and stress the responsibility for critical response to any group.

It is nonetheless important to be clear in the university as to what constitutes a problem, and thus when a university might want to step in. The most important criteria for intervention are harassment, and interference with effective university work. Being contacted several times in the day by phone, for instance, is a good example of harassment which can be dealt with by law. Where universities have attempted a blanket ban this has simply led to publicity for the group, which has fostered claims of persecution.

There are many organizations which claim expertise in this area. However, two stand out:

- INFORM (inform@lse.ac.uk). Based at the London School of Economics, this provides a cool and objective view of NRMs. They recognize that problems are often two-sided. Hence, the reaction to friends and family can often say more about the family relationships than about the 'evil' of any cult. They keep a very good database of all NRMs.
- Reachout Trust (publs@reachouttrust.org). This is an evangelical organization that focuses on doctrine as well as practice. It is a very good group to host in relation to the Christian Union, in that it clearly shows how the theology of the NRM differs from the CU.

Advocacy

A Chinese postgraduate student had major problems by the end of her second year. Her English had not developed well enough, and while she was producing some work it was not of sufficient standard. She had been warned of this by her supervisor, and this had led to the student feeling that she had lost face. As the relationship continued she began to feel that she was being persecuted, leading to writer's block. After a warning she was finally called to a formal meeting with the head of department, the post-graduate coordinator, and her supervisor.

In this case there were no clear rights and wrongs. The student had been told early of the requirements in terms of language; the supervisor was under some pressure and had not perhaps given her enough time. When the student, a non-Christian, came to the chaplain it was to try to get him to champion her cause and to help her to prove the bad intentions of the supervisor and department as a whole. The chaplain helped her to reflect on the whole situation, and obtained her permission to speak with the department on her behalf. This was to demonstrate that others were interested in the case, and that this interest was not adversarial. The chaplain then accompanied the student to the formal meeting. Given the student's poor level of confidence this was essential. The result was that the student was given three months to suspend her work, to work solely on her English and to receive close support that would help her through her crisis of confidence. She would then restart with a new supervisor who would negotiate a clear learning contract.

There were prophetic issues in this case, not least about the needs of postgraduate international students. These were taken up with the postgraduate office. The immediate concern, however, was not with the rights and wrongs, but rather to ensure that the student received proper treatment and the most effective support.

As with prophecy, advocacy is practised by many different groups on campus. On the whole, departments encourage students to bring someone with them to formal meetings. The key group representing students in this way is the student union. It has the legal back-up to make sure that students' rights are respected. Hence, even when the student is clearly in the wrong, as in cases of plagiarism, representation ensures a respectful and appropriate outcome.

It is useful for the chaplain at least to get to know the head of the office that deals with discipline and appeals. This further enables the gap between discipline and pastoral care to be creatively managed, thus reinforcing advocacy as a key part of this process.

Conclusion

Prophecy is critical to the ministry of chaplaincy. It is part of the integrity of the chaplain that issues of justice and ethics should not be sidestepped. The real question then is how it should be done. This chapter has suggested that it should be done with wisdom and care and done together, without as far as possible drawing attention to itself. In all this, prophecy connects organically to networking, pastoral care and indeed to teaching. Teaching in the curriculum itself, as we shall now see, can become a place of prophecy, one in which the stress is on enabling others to be prophetic (Robinson 1994).

References

Armstrong, J., Dixon, R. and Robinson, S., *The Decision Makers: ethics for engineers,* Thomas Telford, London, 1999.

Barker, E., *New Religious Movements*, HMSO, London, 1995.

Gill, R., *Prophecy and Paxis*, Gill and Macmillan, London, 1981.

Grainger, R., *Watching for Wings*, Darton, Longman and Todd, London, 1979.

Lamdin, K., 'Professional Issues', in Legood, G. (ed.), *Chaplaincy,* Cassell, London, 1999.

Longbottom, F., 'Paper on chaplaincy in psychiatry and mental handicap' in *A Handbook of Hospital Chaplaincy*, Hospital Chaplaincies' Council, London, 1987.

Pattison, S., *Pastoral Care and Liberation Theology*, Cambridge University Press, Cambridge, 1993.

Robinson, S., 'Modern Business Ethics and Prophecy', *Crucible,* Oct–Dec 1994, pp. 189–203.

Faith in the Curriculum

Halfway through the three-hour seminar on engineering and ethical decision-making, the chaplain turned back to the overhead and asked the class of about 120 students, 'And what else would you have in a moral decision-making process?' It was a warm day and they were all ready for the coffee break. So when the chaplain heard a shout from the back of the class, 'doctrine!', he didn't really take it in. Indeed, for a moment he thought he was back at theological college . . . those glorious days when you could watch cricket at the Parks and discuss theology with the keen theological students of Oxford.

Just in time he woke up to the enormity of the situation and turned to face the class. There sat not an enthusiastic Christian but a rather matter-of-fact Muslim student. The chaplain asked the student to clarify what he meant. The student carefully noted how doctrine was the basic life meaning that he found in his religion, and how his view of judgement at the end of time affected how he would take ethical decisions as a professional engineer. The beginnings of a dialogue on integrity and the relationship of private and professional ethics and world-views were then swiftly interrupted by a keen evangelical Christian. A former member of the CU executive, he noted how he too had a doctrine and how this affected his decision-making. An atheist sprang to the attack at this point, wondering whether he was in an engineering seminar or religious studies class, 'It is surely not relevant to talk about all this.' Another atheist then stood up and said, 'I'm an atheist, but I have my doctrine, something about the belief system and world-view that underpins my life, I can't see how they don't affect my professional practice.'

There followed an intense 30-minute debate, involving several students, on the values behind professional values, about different life meaning and the ground, of faith, be that theistic or not.

The curriculum has often been seen as a dangerous, mysterious place where chaplains should not venture, unless they happen to be scholars or fellows, qualified curriculum guides of one form or another. The traditional model of HE chaplaincy was of the academic fellow who was also the pastoral heart of the college. In a postmodern HE world the situation is very different (Robinson and Benwell 2000). Not only are values of the Church explicitly not shared by HE institutions, but there is also an increased sense of professionalization in teaching which makes it clear that the curriculum is not a place for either blinkered evangelists or well-meaning amateurs. For the chaplain this seems to give two alternatives: either you come with tried and tested academic expertise, or you leave the curriculum well alone.

This chapter will suggest that the curriculum is an important and natural place for the chaplain to be, and that while it is important to have some academic expertise on the chaplaincy team you do not have to be an established academic to be involved in curriculum work as part of a team. The curriculum is not a monolith set in stone but is rather constantly evolving, often expressing new objectives, such as the development of skills for employability. Moreover, a significant part of the curriculum is concerned with education and training for professional practice, something which invites reflection beyond the narrow confines of any theoretical discipline. The chaplain is in a unique position both to provide different perspectives in established practice-based modules and to generate and develop new curriculum initiatives which enable spiritual, pastoral and ethical reflection and dialogue in collaboration with different departments and agencies. Bridges in this situation can be built between and within departments, between agencies, between departments and the wider community.

The chapter will detail six ways in which the chaplain can contribute to the curriculum and in which curriculum involvement can enhance the role of the chaplain:

- In the traditional curriculum as teacher.
- In the professional curriculum as teacher and facilitator.
- In the developing curriculum as teacher and facilitator.
- In curriculum networks as facilitator and coordinator.

- In Further Education.
- In the fringe curriculum, as teacher, coordinator or student.

These are not exhaustive or mutually exclusive.

Traditional Curriculum

If the chaplain has teaching expertise she can operate in whatever discipline this is in. This could be seen as simply the chaplain following her particular area of research and interest, in the same way that a parish priest might focus on her study day. There are many examples of parish priests in university towns who do just this, teaching two or three hours a week.

A few chaplains have a teaching position formally tied to their job. Where this is not so it is possible to negotiate with a department to get involved. This might be as paid part-time, or honorary lecturer. The other route into teaching might be via a PhD. For most chaplains this would be in the department of theology, but others have become involved in areas related to previous jobs, such as law, medicine or engineering.

Too much involvement in formal teaching can affect the rest of chaplaincy work.

However, some involvement gives a foothold, a bridge from which to build networks. Many academics feel that the academic chaplain can identify more easily with their role, their pressures and the central concerns of Higher Education. Hence, such a chaplain can develop trust with staff very quickly.

This bridge might involve several possibilities:

- Further networking with staff, including Christian staff.
- Setting up a pastoral network. Often the staff in a department – especially the support staff – will refer students with problems to the chaplain who has the profile in that department. This is good for the department, because it gives them an extra pastoral care dimension, and for the chaplain because the pastoral role is clarified in practice.
- Providing courses that enable reflection beyond a narrow view of the discipline. This can be made even more effective through the chaplain being part of interdisciplinary centres. Business and professional ethics centres, for instance, might take in philosophy,

theology, law, business, economics, engineering, medicine and nursing. Such networks enable outreach and critical dialogue.

While the chaplain's academic skills are the way into the formal curriculum it may be that her professional experience is also a way in. For instance, some departments of theology use chaplains (HE, FE, prison and healthcare) in their pastoral theology courses.

The Professional Curriculum

In recent years a number of important developments have influenced teaching and learning in disciplines related to the professions and in the wider developing curriculum:

- There is an increased stress on transferable skills, a holistic view of learning, and the development of reflective practice. This has even extended beyond skills to attention to attitude, qualities and even virtues (Robinson and Dixon 1997, Carter 1985, Megone and Robinson 2002), and includes awareness and concern for the global community (Collins 2003).
- The continued stress on learner-centred learning (Rogers 1983). This stresses the importance of self-directed learning, through which the student develops autonomy.
- The continued stress, especially in the professions such as engineering, healthcare and medicine, on team teaching and the involvement of tutors who can bring a different perspective to the course. Courses for engineers have frequently brought in members of the industry, the community and of other disciplines to provide contrasting and critical perspectives on practice, purpose and accountability. Above all it enables the development of holistic thinking and awareness beyond the narrow confines of discipline or profession.

In the light of such concerns many schools and faculties welcome an interest from chaplains. Work in two areas shows how chaplains can become involved in the area of professional education.

Ethics and Engineering

Since the late 1990s there has been increased concern in all branches
of engineering about professional ethics, including the development
of various codes of ethics (Armstrong, Dixon and Robinson 1999).
This provides the opportunity to work with departments in a range
of possible ways, from single lectures on ethics to parts of a module,
to a team-taught full module covering all aspects of engineering.
Importantly none of this imposes a particular perspective but rather
enables context-specific and student-centred reflection on method.
This in turn provides a framework for effective reflection on ethical
meaning, the values behind the values. An example of this process is
summarized below.

Session One

A case study of a student engineers' project in the rainforests of
Colombia (see Armstrong, Dixon and Robinson 1999 for details).
Small groups study this, focusing on practice and therefore
method. The small groups feed back their ethical methodology in
the case.

Session Two

The whole group brings together a class methodology and examines each stage, and what it means and involves in practice.
   The usual method stages are:

- Data gathering.
- Value clarification.
- Stakeholder analysis.
- Responsibility analysis of each stakeholder.
- Analysis of possible outcomes.
- Decision in the light of values and context limitations.

Session Three

A case study on professional responsibility. This can focus on
whistleblowing cases such as the Challenger disaster (Megone and
Robinson 2002). Small groups analyse the management culture

and list what they see as the different responsibilities and how they might be fulfilled.

Session Four

Via the concept of responsibility as a virtue this focuses on professional virtues. Carter's taxonomy (1985) is analysed. This taxonomy looks at the connection between knowledge, skills and qualities, and from an engineering perspective notes the importance of 'spiritual qualities'. Such qualities include an awareness and appreciation of the other and the capacity to respond. The concept of inclusive responsibility is considered as the basis of ethics (Bauman 1993).

The emphasis on method and context in such approaches makes them very appropriate for professional practice. At the same time they provide a speedy way of getting into underlying questions. This often occurs at the point of value clarification. Sometimes this is simply an agreement about the obvious, with major principles such as equality of freedom agreed on. At other times it can lead to values contrasts such as the different world-views discussed in the story at the beginning of this chapter. In the above example, this raised major contrasting and conflicting values, including very different cultural views of death, spiritual values and the importance of community in contrast to modern Western approaches to health. It is precisely at the point of value contrasts and conflicts that the class is invited to consider what the basis of these values are, how they might justify them and handle the conflict. For some the conflict emerges between personal and professional values. For others this leads to questions of power conflicts amongst the other stakeholders. The aim then is to give the student the responsibility for analysing these values and thus for holding and dealing with values in practice. The stress on method helps them to learn how to think ethically quickly.

Another pedagogical approach is through role play, such as an enquiry into a proposed building of a road through an area of ecological importance. Such role plays can extend to half a day or even a whole day, with the effect of engaging the affective as well as the cognitive side of the professional.

Spirituality, Medicine and Healthcare

Medical schools distinguish between the core curriculum and the special study modules (SSM). The core curriculum deals with 'the central kernel of competence which each and every medical student is expected to acquire by the time they leave medical school' (SSM Student Manual, University of Leeds, 2001, p. 5). The SSM has knowledge objectives which are 'deeper' and 'broader' than the core curriculum. Since 1963 the General Medical Council has been concerned about the 'overloading of the curriculum' and the need to provide opportunities for 'self-education'. In 1994 it agreed to the recommendation that up to a third of the undergraduate teaching programme be devoted to special study modules.

Its aims are:

- To equip students for a future of self-directed learning.
- To develop essential transferable skills such as information gathering, communication and presentation skills, problem solving and critical reasoning.
- To develop appropriate attitudes of self-motivation, and self evaluation, together with an understanding of the importance of active learning.
- To allow students to extend their knowledge and understanding in subject areas of their choice.

(SSM Student Manual, University of Leeds, 2001)

The modules target specific skills and attitudes rather than facts. Perhaps most importantly they stress learning as an active experience.

Elective modules for one part of the SSM include:

- An introduction to the theory and practice of counselling.
- Community-based projects.
- Teaching skills for undergraduate students.
- Working together: being part of the healthcare team.

The SSM programme makes it clear that a good honours degree cannot be achieved without excellent work in both core and SSM curricula. There are options within the SSMs, though ethics is mandatory.

The key factor of these courses is the development of the reflective practitioner. Hence, through reflection a great deal of time is spent on the purposes and underlying values of the profession.

Chaplains can become involved at all levels of the SSM. This benefits both chaplaincy and the school of medicine. The chaplaincy becomes part of a reflective process critical to the professional development of the students. The school widens dialogue and reflection in creative ways. In Leeds this has led to the development of a module in spirituality and medicine and the development of several different research topics on that theme. The module includes:

- Definitions of spirituality and how they relate to health.
- How spirituality relates to mental health.
- Spirituality and therapy.
- Spirituality and trauma.
- Spirituality and death.
- Spirituality and the identity of the healthcare professions.
- Assessment of spiritual need.

Once again, as with traditional teaching, this can lead to the development and affirmation of many different networks. In medicine there is the Christian Medical Fellowship, as well as many Christian medical staff members, all of which can be linked with. Also, there are existing medical ethics networks which the chaplain can become part of, not least through involvement in seminar work. This work here can interrelate with spirituality modules. Further networking can occur through including hospital chaplains in the delivery of the courses, drawing on their skills and experience and setting up links with the future doctors.

Healthcare studies and in particular nursing have strong professional as well as educational drivers to include not only ethics but also spirituality in the curriculum (Robinson, Kendrick and Brown 2003). This has lead to the development of spirituality and healthcare modules delivered by chaplains in collaboration with the departmental staff.

The Developing Curriculum

There is now a whole aspect of the curriculum which is focused on the development of skills, the development of the person and employability. This began through the exploratory work of Enterprise in Higher Education, in which Government money was made available to develop imaginative courses (Robinson 1996).

This has led to the development of accredited and elective central skills modules, aiming to focus on vocational skills as part of the curriculum. Once more then the driver for such courses is work application, and this opens up courses run by agencies as diverse as the careers office and student counselling. One such course is run by Student Action, a student community volunteer society, in co-ordination with the Department of Continuing Education. It includes the theories and issues underlying the process of volunteering, the skills necessary for voluntary work, the stages of volunteer development and the effect of voluntary work on the community.

The chaplaincy fits easily into such a marketplace of electives. One example of what can be done is the Lifeskills and Spirituality course at the University of Leeds. This is summarized below.

Lifeskills and Spirituality

The course runs over two semesters, and is capable of being divided into two short modules involves:

Defining spirituality

This invites wide ranging reflection on the meaning of spirituality, arriving at a working definition which is tested throughout the course.

Spirituality is then distinguished from religion, psychology and ethics, and the students are invited to reflect (confidentially) on their own spirituality through working out a life map or values history.

Spirituality and Health

The relationship of spirituality to health and well-being is explored. This leads to an examination of the part spirituality can play in the healing process, and an identification of the key skills involved. The focus is on empathy as a spiritual skill and the underlying attitude of unconditional care, especially in terms of agape.

This is developed in relation to hope, faith, purpose and reconciliation and forgiveness, culminating in the idea of *shalom*.

All this is applied to death, dying and bereavement.

Conflict Resolution

The dynamics of forgiveness and reconciliation are developed in relation to the skills of conflict resolution, including contexts such as the family.

Work

The nature of work in terms of purpose, vocation, hope and faith is examined. How this ties in with professional decision-making and management is then examined, along with the underlying skills. This includes work culture and whistleblowing.

Community

Different kinds of community, how they learn and develop identity and meaning, are examined. The different meanings of these communities are tested and the underlying skills of community development in a postmodern age articulated.

Global Issues

Spirituality and awareness of global issues, especially poverty and the care of the environment, are developed and connected to everyday life, including issues about multinational corporations and state responsibility.

The Divine

Because a significant part of the course is seminars where the different spiritual narratives of the students are shared, the Divine is not absent up to this point. However, thoughts about the transcendent other are drawn together at the end, not least issues about how we can know such an 'other', or even talk about him.

Once again this module is student-centred, enabling reflection on the 'other' (be that self, other person, group, environment or the divine), on how we respond to the other, and on how we generate significant life meaning for ourselves and others through those relationships. Precisely because such reflection does not shirk the conflicts in ideas and feelings that might arise, it enables dialogue which works through to criteria for challenging different spiritualities, not least as to whether they are healthy or not.

The course is assessed by a 4,000-word essay (examining the grasp of theory and application) and by a reflective learning journal (examining how the student connects the ideas to their own spiritual journey). The reflective journal and seminar work are key to building up intertextual dialogue. The journal invites reflection on:

- The seminars, noting what was discussed and critically analysing this.
- The skills and qualities practised.
- How the issues raised connect with their home discipline.
- How the issues connect with their own spirituality and any vocation.
- Any issues that made the student feel uneasy.

The chaplaincy team is responsible for most of the course, but external teachers or members of departments can be brought in for different sections. Particularly fruitful is the possibility of working with chaplains from other sectors, such as healthcare, industry and prisons. Also useful is to have an industrial consultant who can reflect on how the course ties in to work issues.

Curriculum Networking

Increasingly departments are being asked to reflect on the global perspective of their courses. The Toyne Report, for instance, recommended that, 'Responsible Global Citizenship should be recognized as a desired learning outcome; "Enabling responsible citizenship" should be recognized as a core business of learning institutions and a legitimate purpose of lifetime learning' (Khan 1996). While core modules can be organized on this theme this also has a clear relevance to most vocational courses. The overview of this is something that chaplaincy is ideally placed to facilitate and accompany. Through the pioneering work of Gwen Collins, Leeds Metropolitan University has developed a Global Perspectives Network, with academic, administrative and support staff from all departments. It aims 'to stimulate debate, to share ideas and materials across Faculties, and to contribute to the formulation of university policy' (Collins 2003).

Such a network then directly affects the curriculum, but can also affect the policy of the university. At its centre is a global spirituality which sets out 'global perspectives', including how they can be embedded in the curriculum, how students will benefit from such perspectives and what academics would be aiming for, summed up as follows:

What are global perspectives?

1 A degree in which global perspectives are embedded:
   • Draws examples from a wide variety of human experience.
   • Enables students to grow in understanding of global realities.
   • Takes seriously issues of global responsibility.
   • Recognizes that these issues impact on professionals in all disciplines.
2 Students who benefit from such an education will have the opportunity to:
   • Develop cross-cultural awareness.
   • Appreciate and celebrate diversity.
   • Understand the wider global context in which they will work.
   • Learn how they can act with others to bring about change.

3 Academics who incorporate global perspectives into their
  work:
  • Encourage students to question the status quo.
  • Recognize that no course, however technical, is value free.
  • Understand the imbalances within which their own profes-
    sions or disciplines are set.
  • Value research opportunities that contribute to the construc-
    tion of a sustainable and equitable future.

(Collins 2003)

An invaluable part of any curriculum network strategy can be work-
based ministers. They may already have detailed knowledge of
the department and the curriculum possibilities, and can quickly
develop appropriate modules.

Further Education

Curriculum involvement is very relevant to FE. In fact FE has
pioneered different approaches to it. As early as 1992 a report from
Clifford Jenkins defined the churches' mission in this area as:

> To contribute to the pursuit of excellence in FE and have a
> concern for the spiritual, moral and personal values being com-
> municated and developed through the whole curriculum and
> other aspects of college life (Churches' Further Education Cur-
> riculum Working Group 1996).

This was later echoed by recommendations 181 and 182 of the
Dearing Report, which looked to the relevance of spiritual and
moral issues in particular subjects. The Churches' Further Education Curriculum Working Group notes many areas where this can
be developed, including:

• Biology, in the areas of genes and genetic engineering, reproduc-
  tion and contraception, and AIDS.
• Geography, with the whole range of global issues.
• Student development programmes, including decision-making
  skills and human development – from birth to death.

The pioneering work of FE chaplains has demonstrated clearly how chaplaincy can enable spiritual and moral dialogue in most areas of the curriculum.

Fringe Curriculum

In addition to the traditional and developing curriculum there are a number of different ways in which chaplains can be involved in the non-formal or fringe curriculum.

- *Personal development modules and seminars.* The student union or student support services quite often offer short courses in personal development of different kinds, such as developing the skills of befriending. This is primarily a network for students who might want to develop some aspects of themselves. Chaplaincy can usefully be a part of such a network, with short courses available to all students, such as one on different kinds of spiritual and devotional techniques, or vocation.
- *Chaplaincy outreach programmes.* These are designed to pick up controversial issues on campus and develop reflection and debate. This may mean the chaplaincy setting up speakers they may not always agree with. Such one-off sessions can be set up in collaboration with departments.
- *Participating in regular public lectures and seminars.* At one level this involves monitoring the occasional lectures and seminars in the university and ensuring that there is a chaplain at the ones which are most likely to enable fruitful dialogue.

Chaplains may also enter the curriculum not as providers but as consumers. This can range from the conventional approach of doing an MA in theology, to the chaplain with artistic experience doing the life-drawing module. This in turn provides the possibility of connecting to other quite different networks. It also helps the chaplain to identify with the present issues in the experiences of students.

Other Areas

Many other areas can be explored, not least science, social sciences, politics and English. Where it is not immediately clear how spirituality might be relevant to a department or faculty then setting up a one-off lecture with an eminent visiting speaker might help possibilities to be explored.

Relations with Theology

Some of the modules described above could be done in collaboration with theology. However, this is not necessary. Theology and religious studies might see themselves as distinct from this approach.

Where there is no department of theology there is the possibility of the chaplaincy taking over some of its role, becoming a distinct centre of theological reflection or applied theology. However, the effort needed to maintain such a centre could detract from other aspects of chaplaincy.

Midwife or Companion?

It is possible to see the chaplain's role in such work with departments or networks as simply the midwife, who moves out of the scene once the module is ready. In some contexts that might be the right action. However, while the chaplain should not retain control of any course her perspective can remain of great value to the department and point to continued collaboration in course delivery. The chaplain then still maintains her interest in continuing reflection, and is perhaps better seen as the skilled companion in this process.

Conclusion

There are many advantages to using curriculum involvement in any of the ways noted above:

- It increases chaplaincy networking and profiling in a major way.
- It provides the basis for mission as dialogue, through reflection on life meaning and how this relates to learning and decision-making

in practice. It provides the kind of reflection that Williams (2004) points to and the conversations that Ford (1999) extols, both of which enable a transcendent perspective in teaching and research.

• It greatly increases the numbers of students in contact with chaplains. This applies even when the contact is one lecture as part of a module. One chaplain, for instance, gave the same lecture on spirituality to four healthcare and engineering classes over four weeks, speaking to a total number of over 1,000 students.

• It provides ways of extending ethical and spiritual dialogue beyond the local context, leading in some cases to publications (Armstrong, Dixon and Robinson 1999; Robinson, Kendrick and Brown 2003).

It is important not to see this as simply an alternative or exclusive approach to chaplaincy. Through effective teamwork, curriculum involvement can be balanced with pastoral care and attention to worship. Effective networking with departments and with other student support networks ensures that involvement is appropriate and not too demanding.

Work with departments may require careful handling of resources. It can also contribute to resources. Where the chaplaincy is delivering a course for the central curriculum this can provide income that can cover any educational resources needed, including buying in tutors for specialist areas.

Many chaplains are reluctant to become involved in these areas because they do not feel qualified. However, if the team has a development plan then it is possible to aim to include in the team one person with some experience of university teaching and/or research. This would demonstrate to the university how seriously the churches take this mission. In addition the ongoing training of chaplains can ensure that chaplains who want to develop this ministry can attend university training courses on pedagogy. The traditionalist model demanded that only chaplains with academic qualifications should be involved in teaching. The involvement in some modules is often not of that type, focusing rather on skills development and adult education, very much part of student ministry.

Summary

Steps to Curriculum involvement:

In Departments

1 Get to know the department, its issues, concerns, professional drivers, key and responsive members. Most of this information can be gleaned from a couple of meetings with the head of department and other colleagues.
2 Test out the openness of the department to chaplaincy involvement. Explore a realistic response, involving initially brief involvement. Review that work with the course leader at the end of the academic year, with a view to development.
3 Explore the possibilities of joint papers.

From Chaplaincy

1 Locate the appropriate pro-vice-chancellor and discuss the course options.
2 Where there is a department of theology discuss the possibility of the module being supported by them.
3 Send in an application to the appropriate teaching and learning committee, setting out objectives and learning outcomes. This provides a rigorous basis for the course and is, in any case, good discipline for the chaplaincy team.
4 Set up an academic board within the chaplaincy that can oversee the courses. This can include chaplains and any consultants, from industry or from other departments.

Where possible the different aspects of curriculum involvement and even of other chaplaincy programmes could be co-ordinated. For instance, in the middle of a course of Spirituality and Healthcare a one-off major public lecture on Christian Spirituality and Health.

References

Armstrong, J., Dixon, R. and Robinson, S., *The Decision Makers*, Thomas Telford, London, 1999.

Bauman, Z., *Postmodern Ethics*, Oxford University Press, Oxford, 1993.

Carter, R., 'A taxonomy of objectives for professional education', *Studies in Higher Education* 10 (2), 1985, pp. 135–49.

Churches' Further Education Curriculum Group, *Student Entitlement to Spiritual, Moral and Personal Values in the FE Curriculum*, Methodist Church Division of Education and Youth, London, 1996.

Collins, G., *Going Global at Leeds Metropolitan University*, a discussion document from the Global Perspectives Network, January 2003.

Ford, D., 'God and the University: What can we communicate?' Paper given to the National Convention on Christian Ministry in Higher Education, High Lea, Hoddesden, 1999.

Khan, S., *Environmental Responsibility: A Review of the Toyne Report*, DfEE, Welsh Office, Dept of the Environment, 1996, p.13.

Megone, C. and Robinson, S. (eds), *Case Histories in Business Ethics*, Routledge, London, 2002.

Robinson, S., 'To Boldy Go: A tale of spiritual enterprise in Higher Education', *Crucible,* Jan–Mar 1996, pp. 12–19.

Robinson, S., and Benwell, M., 'Christian Chaplaincy in the Postmodern University', *Modern Believing* 41 (1), 1999.

Robinson, S. and Dixon, R., 'The Professional Engineer: Virtues and Learning', *Science and Engineering Ethics* 3(3), 1997, pp. 339–48.

Robinson, S., Kendrick, K. and Brown, A., *Spirituality and the practice of Healthcare*, Palgrave Macmillan, Basingstoke, 2003.

Rogers, C., *Freedom to Learn*, Merrill, Columbus, 1983.

SSM, *SSM Student Manual*, University of Leeds, Leeds, 2001.

Williams, R., 'Faith in the University', in Katalushi, C. and Robinson, S. (eds), *Values in Higher Education*, University of Leeds Press, Leeds, 2004.

Conclusions

Why God Never Received Tenure at any University

1 He has only one major publication.
2 It was in Hebrew.
3 It had no references.
4 It wasn't published in a refereed journal.
5 Some even doubt he wrote it himself.
6 It may be true that he created the world but what has he done since?
7 The scientific community had a hard time replicating his results.
8 He never applied to the ethics board for permission to use humans.
9 He rarely came to class, just telling his students to read the Book.
10 He expelled his first two students for learning.
11 Although there were only ten requirements most students failed his tests.
12 His office hours were infrequent and usually held on a mountain top.

Despite this assessment of God in Higher and Further Education, these now form areas which are potentially open to God as few others. With the Government aim of involving half of 18–30 year olds in Higher Education within the next few years, and with Further Education reaching over four million people, the opportunities for mission and ministry to students have never been so great. The majority of those students are experiencing transition, be that late adolescence or middle age change, questioning previous life-scripts and searching for life meaning that illuminates change. If ever there was a time and place for the Church to be there and enable reflection that connects meaning and experience this is it.

This book has suggested that the mission to students should be:

- *Dialogic*. Chaplaincy enables the Christian narrative to be articulated but also enables real dialogue in the first place. This demands a mission of empathy, in which Christians listen to the meaning of lives as well as share our insights.
- *Collaborative*. With teamwork and networks the conversation can move out far beyond any sense of the Church as club.
- *Holistic*. The conversation is with the whole person, and the whole community. Hence, the concern of student ministry is as much about the spirituality of the educational institution as the person (Jenkins 1998).
- *Integrated*. All the different parts of ministry, however they are defined, are connected in practice. Prophetic work links to pastoral work, challenging the unhealthy patterns of behaviour that can underpin any institution or any individual life. Teaching links to prophecy and can often in turn link to pastoral care. Worship stands at the base of the conversation looking both to pastoral care and prophecy.

This is a mission that should know the culture with which it is in conversation intimately. It understands the issues of, for instance, transferable skills and will engage them in conversation about qualities and virtues and community. As such it will pick up in practice all the theology of community from Tawney to Hauerwas, and take this beyond the confines of the Church.

There are, however, several problems:

- Money in all the churches is limited. In that situation the chaplain is usually the first one to go.

- The Church's links with the sector are not always firmly established. Perhaps most importantly the Church has not fully begun to comprehend how work with students fits in with the rest of the ministry and mission. Hence, it is often not part of any mission strategy.
- Universities and FE colleges often do not really understand what chaplains are about. Some are fearful of religion and the possible flashpoints. All want to find ways of relating that are both safe and creative.
- Chaplaincy has been inconsistent and non-collaborative in the past. The model has been mostly a parish one that assumes territorial continuity while at the same time appointing chaplains for a relatively short time, leading to frequently changing approaches to the ministry.

The first of these problems demands flexibility and openness to different possibilities. Yes, finances are desperate in many areas. However, it is possible to explore greater use of work-based ministers, greater collaboration with local churches, and closer work with staff and students. It is precisely this kind of networking that can develop creative responses. Greater collaboration with universities in the curriculum and through SLAs can also produce different sources of income. Indeed, the more the Church is in conversation with the sector, and the more the role of chaplain is articulated, the more institutions might finance parts of chaplaincy.

The second problem demands clear objectives in a mission strategy. All too often the sector and parish ministries have been seen to be separate and not connected. Avis (1999) dares to consider that it might even be important to make HE chaplaincy a priority, working in co-ordination with local churches.

The third problem demands creative contract work. The Church's theology of contract has been almost non-existent. Yes, the base of our faith is covenantal, not contractual, but that covenant is hard actually to set in practice without contract, without clarifying just what we are doing, both for the Church and the institutions. This is a vital element in developing trust with the sector as a whole and the local institutions in particular.

The fourth demands a view of chaplaincy which is team based. This is where the key importance of ecumenism stands out, providing a team with objectives that are greater than any group's or individual's contribution. This level of commitment over time also works against the short-termist and fragmented approach. In all this the Church has to give greater stress to the development of teams, enabling the team to be a learning organization, encouraging the development of reflective practice, and ensuring long-term support.

In the light of all this there can be greater confidence about what it means to be a competent chaplain or student worker. Practice has tended to assume that the key qualities and skills of the ordained clergy can be transferred easily to chaplaincy. This is now being seriously questioned; first, because ordination is not necessary for the greater part of the chaplaincy task. Second, the knowledge and skills required for practice in this sector, outlined in this book, are focused very differently from parish work.

The Integrity of Chaplaincy

There are those who fear that chaplaincy is in danger of 'going native', of simply becoming a part of the institution and thus no longer part of the cutting edge of the Church's mission. In such a situation there is a real question about whether the Church should pay for what, it is feared, might amount to a social worker with a concern for spirituality. Pattison (2001), reflecting on healthcare chaplaincy, argues that the concern for modern spiritualities sets up a lowest common denominator and can lead the Christian chaplain to forget that she has a clear narrative centred on spirit with a capital S. Behind all this seems to be a fear of losing the Christian identity. There are several problems with this:

- The majority of students do not have any sense of the spiritual, a sense of that which transcends the self. It is very hard to speak of the Spirit without having a broader concept of the spiritual in which to frame it. That framework was there 2000 years ago, because everyone was seeking to find some form of spiritual meaning in life. Today, there is no single one, and for many none. The chaplain therefore has to enable the student to reflect on life meaning, within which a real conversation about different spiritualities can take place.
- The Christian faith has a history of imperialism, and claims for a privileged narrative. In post-compulsory education there can be

no such privilege. It would also be wrong to engage the sector in conversation with the hidden agenda of using this to simply gain converts.

• Chaplaincy is essentially a dual ministry. It seeks to enable narrative and conversation as well as share its own narrative. It is perfectly possible to have conversation, in the curriculum, through pastoral care and so on, which is non-directive, and at the same time, in another context such as worship or public lectures, to have an approach that proclaims of the Christian narrative very directly. In other words the chaplaincy can retain its integrity without having to say the same thing in all contexts.

Meaning in Higher and Further Education

The more the Church ensures a significant network in post-compulsory education, the more it can contribute to the development of and reflection on meaning and values in that sector. This may mean supporting certain widely held values and critiquing others. Values which the Church can support include:

• Equality of opportunity and resources through widening participation.
• The development of the whole person, including qualities and skills. The question of transferable skills.
• The development of responsibility and accountability in resource management.
• The importance of plurality. Without this tolerance and freedom begin to erode. The university can be at the centre of this for the wider community.
• The stress on academic freedom as the basis of truth and knowledge.

This is all part of the dialogue with the sector which has a lot to teach the Church. Equally the Church has much to say to HE and FE, including:

• A critique of the customer revolution and the simplistic view of autonomy.
• Stress on working together – community and purpose – over and against simply rights or consumer approaches.

- Stress on social responsibility and the part that HE and FE play in the local and global community.

Jenkins (1988) suggests that the Christian Church should argue for all the different purposes of the university and support post-compulsory education as a place of critique, where it is safe to challenge all assertions of truth, including the political. Hence, any chaplaincy should embody values such as truthfulness, transparency, faithfulness, hope, community and love.

Such dialogues as this contribute towards the spirituality of post-compulsory education, helping the institution itself to reflect further on meaning and need on campus and beyond.

National Perspectives

If the chaplaincy can contribute to reflection on the campus then the churches as a whole can contribute to meaning and debate in this sector at a national level. This can occur partly through the national advisors on chaplaincy and partly through the systems that each church has for connecting to political thinking. It is important for the chaplain to make use of these networks and contribute to them.

A national perspective on chaplaincy in post-compulsory education is also important, such that institutions across the country can recognize what chaplaincy has to offer and how they can relate. This means ensuring that aims, objectives and standards are shared by chaplains across the country. This does not mean professionalizing chaplaincy in such a way that it simply becomes another agency of HE or FE. It rather points to a professionalization that seeks to ensure that the theology outlined in this book is applied systematically and responsively across the sector, with the practitioners accountable for that application to church, academic institution, and co-workers.

Job Description

I have purposely left this to the end. If it is to have any clarity then it needs to take into account the qualities, skills and knowledge required to develop the priestly, pastoral and prophetic work of student ministry. These are common to all appointments. In addition the local situation will affect any job description, not least in terms of procedure and accountability. This will vary greatly, depending upon whether the university or college appoints its own chaplains or they are appointed by the Church. Some will involve well-developed ecumenical teams with particular needs, others will be largely single-handed. Either way it is important to establish expectations with all the different parties.

Above all the job description should ensure that the chaplain is focused on the mission statement of the team, and upon the widest possible network of mission to students.

References

Avis, P., 'Towards a Theology of Sector Ministry', in Legood, G. (ed.), *Chaplaincy*, Cassell, London, 1999, pp. 3–14.

Jenkins, D., 'What is the Purpose of a University – and what light does Christian faith shed on this question?', *Studies in Higher Education* 13 (3), 1988, pp. 239–47.

Jenkins, C., *Developing a Spirituality Policy for Further Education Sector Colleges*, Church of England Board of Education, 1998.

Pattison, S., 'Dumbing Down the Spirit', in Orchard, H. (ed.), *Spirituality in Health Care Contexts*, Jessica Kingsley, London, 2001, pp. 33–46.

Appendix

Universities

This appendix looks briefly at the history of the university, primarily in the UK and begins to focus on what the university is. It ends with a reflection on the place of religion in Higher and Further Education and developments in chaplaincy.

The Medieval University

In 1850 the life of Oxford was dominated by the Established Church. Bebbington reflects that,

> all heads of house except one were in the Anglican ministry; virtually all tutors were clergymen; and about 80 per cent of undergraduates were intending to pursue a clerical career. Students had to subscribe to the Thirty-Nine Articles of the Church of England on admission to the university; they took an obligatory test in Greek New Testament and attended compulsory college chapel (Bebbington 1992, 259).

Power, knowledge, learning and the Church were inextricably entwined at the heart of the university system, tracing its origins back to the medieval Christian Church. With the founding of Oxford and Cambridge universities, in 1264 and 1284 respectively, there was a common world-view which formed the basis of learning, community and worship (Jenkins 1988, 242). It would be over 600 years before another English university was founded. Both Oxford and Cambridge added several colleges, but it remained the universities which conferred degrees.

These were not the first universities in Europe, nor, by the fifteenth century, did they remain the only ones in the British Isles.

Bologna and Paris among others were already in place. St Andrews was founded between 1411 and 1413, followed by Glasgow (1451), Aberdeen (1495) and Edinburgh (1583). The first three of these had strong links to Europe, being founded by the Pope. Edinburgh, however, was unique, being a civic foundation, with the Crown giving authority to confer degrees. Soon after, in 1591, Dublin University was founded. Ironically, this was developed on the pattern of Oxford and Cambridge, and until well after the rise of the Irish Republic was exclusively for Anglicans.

Though these universities developed by different routes, on the whole they shared the founding subjects of theology, law and the arts, providing education for the professional classes. There were other stirrings, though, in Edinburgh with the rise of medical sciences. This stress on science eventually gave rise to the modern university, something very much based in mainland Europe.

The Modern University

Gordon Graham characterizes the modern university as 'a non denominational institution in which natural science played a significant part and where theology and history were subject to critical scrutiny' (Graham 2002, 7). In 1694 this was already developing in the University of Halle. The development of the experimental sciences reached a peak in Berlin in the first decade of the nineteenth century.

It did not take long (1827) for the establishment of London University (later University College, London) to follow, in what was, in effect, the first real push for widening participation. It aimed to broaden opportunities for education to occupations beyond the traditional professions and equally importantly to admit Jews, Roman Catholics and Nonconformists. Because of this it was denied a charter and was unable to award degrees. Within four years of this came the reaction of the Establishment with the founding of King's College, which, being Anglican, could, of course, have a charter and confer degrees.

Looking back on this period from the perspective of another wave of widening participation, the attempt of the Anglican Establishment to keep power to itself and thus exclude massive areas of society from Higher Education is extraordinary. By the mid nineteenth century other denominations, the popular press and finally Parliament began to attack this exclusivism. Newman founded the Catholic University in Dublin in 1851. Two Acts, 1852 and 1854, finally brought some reform, enabling access to Oxford and Cambridge for students who were not part of the Church of England, though religious tests were not finally abolished in these universities until 1871.

Alongside this was the expansion of the university system to civic and federal universities. In 1836 London University was established as a federation of colleges, thus finally establishing a fourth university in England (after Durham in 1832) with a totally different character from Oxford and Cambridge. Central to this was provision in 1849 for external as well as internal students. This had the effect of breaking the old patterns of residential education and widening access to Higher Education. Up to this time students who had little means had greater opportunities in Scotland. This federal pattern had some influence, with the founding of the National University of Ireland and the University of Wales. However, the real explosion of Higher Education took place in the latter half of the nineteenth century.

Several factors were involved in this process, including the following:

- The later universities were fuelled by the industrial revolution and in many cases by a real concern for local pride. These were based around the local industries such as textiles (Leeds), food (Birmingham and Liverpool), and tobacco (Bristol).
- Many of these universities represented the challenge of Nonconformity to the control of the Established Church (Thom 1987).

With all this the student population was rising significantly, enhanced by the admission of women in the 1880s. Nonetheless, by the mid twentieth century less than 3 per cent of school leavers went on to university, a very low participation rate compared to America and Canada (Graham 2002, 9).

Concern about this eventually led to the Robbins Report (*Higher Education* 1963). The report recommendations included:

- Increasing the number of university places.

- The creation of a number of new universities. In all, 18 were built, mostly on green field sites, such as Kent, York and Lancaster.
- Developing different, more flexible patterns of degree course, stressing interdisciplinary work.

Between 1968 and 1991 the number of students in Higher Education rose from 200,000 to 360,000 (Higher Education Funding Council England 1994, 1).

The 1960s also saw the rise of the polytechnics. These provided an alternative to universities, with a stress on more vocational courses. By 1991 numbers in this sector had risen to 370,000 (HEFCE 1994, 2). Polytechnics developed strong links with local industry and business. With the Further and Higher Education Act of 1992 the polytechnics all became universities. Virtually overnight the number of universities was doubled, to almost 100, with 20 per cent of the population in England and Wales enrolled in some form of HE course.

Widening participation in HE reached its highpoint with the establishment of the Open University in 1969. By 2003 more than 200,000 people were studying with the Open University. It provides flexible distance learning which enables study in the home or workplace. Almost 80 per cent of its students are in paid employment. It combines this with support from local tutors and summer schools, and happily calls itself, 'Everyone's local university'.

Meanwhile, the end of the twentieth century saw the development of a vision for the University of the Highlands and Islands. Not only is this aiming to provide good distance learning for a region which includes 75 islands as well as the mainland, it also takes the idea of everyone's local university one step further. It aims to nurture the culture and community of the region, with a curriculum that grows from the area's 'unique cultural and environmental heritage' (www.uhi.ac.uk). All of these developments have pioneered the delivery of distance learning, through television and now through e-learning. By 2003 some 160,000 Open University students were online, using the university's email conferencing system.

A further development has been work-based universities. In the 1990s Unipart pioneered this, providing appropriate modules for its entire staff (Megone and Robinson 2002, 140). At the time of writing, the National Health Service is well down the line in developing such a facility.

By 1997 and the Dearing Report, however, there were major questions on the horizon, not least how can the Government afford all this and does the country as such need it?

Government, Finance and Higher Education

Government involvement in Higher Education is nothing new, not least in giving university the power to confer degrees. However, through the twentieth century universities became increasingly dependent upon the Government for their finances. By the 1970s student fees were paid for by local government (and reclaimed from central government), there was a statutory student grant paid by central government via the University Grants Commission, and research funding came via the Research Councils.

With the 1980s there were general cutbacks in all State spending, including HE. Universities, sensing that their future depended upon Government funding, responded with attempts to cut back and restructure. However, widening participation was still a priority. As numbers were exploding, though, resources were not keeping pace. University status for polytechnics, for instance, meant them now entering into direct competition for the same resources as other universities.

Alongside resources there was also the issue of how the standards of all these, sometimes very different, bodies might be maintained. This led to a threefold pattern of government control:

- Higher Education Funding Councils in England, Wales and Scotland. The councils were in charge of funding initiatives for a variety of areas, including student recruitment and retention, teaching and research, and employability. These involved bidding for limited amounts of money.
- The Research Assessment Exercise was set up to review the standards of research and scholarship in university departments. Subject panels of peers from other universities were responsible for this. Once again money was related to this exercise. If, for instance, a department received a lower research rating than the previous exercise it stood to lose income, and with that morale.
- Teaching Quality Assessment involved panels of academic and external representatives from commerce and industry. Their task

Ministry Among Students

was to assess the quality of teaching. The results of these would affect departmental funding. The publication of these results was also something that could affect the students' choice of university and courses. This and the subsequent Quality Assurance Agency have now been replaced by Quality Enhancement. This puts much more stress on internal reviews, conscious that the previous exercises were collapsing under the weight of their own paper trail and that the vast majority of universities were shown to be doing a good job. This assessment has included more than just teaching and learning in the department. The provision of pastoral work, for instance, is examined and commented on.

The consequences of all this have been immense:

1 Universities have become genuinely accountable to the State. It forms the basis of Government inspection comparable to the primary and secondary sectors.
2 It has led to much more pressure in the average academic and support staff life. It involves an increase in productivity of research and greater stress on the effectiveness of teaching. This has led to increased professionalization and with that an increase in administrative detail and tasks. With departments having to manage their own budgets, this has also forced heads of departments into much clearer managerial roles, putting further pressure on them.

Opinions vary as to whether all this is good or bad. Some see it all as a source of stress, diminishing any sense of community or trust. Others see it as the development of proper transparency, leading to creative collaboration.

However, even with these attempts to maintain standards and deal with the finances there were still questions. Resources would still not be enough, and it was not always clear whether students were developing the skills required by future employers. In the light of that the Dearing Report (1997) argued for a stress on life-long learning, focusing on transferable skills. It also recommended that the resources be targeted to widening participation.

The Government, against the recommendations of the Dearing Report, decided to scrap the mandatory Grant and to introduce tuition fees payable by students. Those unable to afford the fees would still be helped. At the time of writing the Government intends to allow universities to charge top-up fees of up to £3,000. The consensus is that most universities will opt to do this. Indeed, the Russell Group, of elite universities, shows every sign of charging even more (Thomson 2003, 1).

Alongside accountability and professionalism is a fast emerging consumerism. The student pays for his education and therefore expects to receive the best. The university is a major business with many jobs depending on it and has to think carefully about consumer care. The effects of this on student culture were explored in Chapter 1.

With the developments of the 1980s and 1990s the question then emerges as to what really is the university in the first place.

What is a University?

Having charted the rise of the university thus far it is now important to ask the question as to what the university actually is. There are two answers, the first is about values and identity and the second is about function. With all the expansion of the university system the picture becomes more confused, with some universities focusing on a narrow curriculum, others offering the broadest possible number of options, some are research centred, some focus largely on teaching and learning, some on vocational training.

Significant reports in this history have tried to articulate that identity. Robbins (*Higher Education* 1963) sees four aims of the university:

- The development of skills.
- Promotion of the general powers of the mind.
- The advancement of learning and search for truth.
- Transmission of a common culture and common standards of citizenship.

Dearing (*National Committee of Enquiry* 1997) also offers four aims:

- To develop the person's potential to be well equipped for work, and to contribute to society.
- To increase knowledge and understanding – for their own sake and for the economy.

- To serve the needs of the economy at all levels.
- To help shape a democratic and civilized society.

Both include a rich variety of values from a utilitarian view of education to belief in education for its own sake. Hence, in addition to any questions of utility, Dearing quotes in his foreword an excerpt from John Masefield's address to the University of Sheffield in 1946. The university,

> is a place where those who hate ignorance may strive to know, where those who perceive truth may strive to make others see, where seekers and learners alike band together in search for knowledge, will honour thought in all its finer ways, will welcome thinkers in distress or in exile, will uphold ever the dignity of thought and learning and will exact standards in these things.

This is a very elevated view of values. However, many universities today would not recognize that idea of the university as applied to them. Many of the more recent universities spend less than 2 per cent of their income on research, and have neither the space nor the time to develop the high-flown dialogue between the few researchers they have and the undergraduates, many of whom live at home and have no inclination to enter into the wider kingdom of ideas. This is not to denigrate such universities. On the contrary, some would argue, including Newman (1983), that a university is primarily a place for teaching, not research.

The truth is that universities have never had a single focus (Jenkins 1988). As Graham points out (2002, 21) the Papal Bull establishing Aberdeen University made it clear that it was for providing both 'the most precious pearl of knowledge', knowledge for its own sake, and training for the professions, in particular the law and the Church. Moreover, it was implicit that in providing for such professions universities were contributing toward civilization per se.

Hence, we can begin to paint a complex picture of what a university is: built up of several elements; something that can only be fleshed out in relation to the context and limitations of the particular university. This might involve many different views of the value of the university, including:

- Barnett argues that the core of university education involves discipline-transcending reflection leading to a fuller understanding of the self. This looks to the development of the rounded person irrespective of occupational utility (Barnett 1990). Williams also has this sense of transcendence and reflection in focusing on the experience of learning about learning, and therefore about how one grows (Williams 2004).

- Writing from an American perspective, Thomas Bender (2004) sees the university as the essential guardian of pluralism. As distinct from providing a safe place to develop, this is more a liberal argument about guarding the right to have and develop one's own value.
- Hardy (1992) sees the university as a means 'whereby society transcends itself', where values are reflected on and transmitted throughout society.
- Escobar and Freire (1994) suggest that the university can act as conscience to society, not just civilizing but 'moralizing' and critiquing society.
- Both Robbins and Dearing are aware of the importance of HE to industry but also the professions, and from this to the wealth an stability of society.
- White (1996) suggests that there is a rich mixture of values in Higher Education. He argues against a view of HE as liberationist, stressing the importance of student preference and thus of the consumerist model of education.
- R. H. Tawney saw post-compulsory education as a critical way of developing equality in the sense of bringing together different classes into 'the kingdom of ideas' (Tawney 1930), and thus developing community. The more recent stress on widening participation is more about equality as equalizing opportunities.

The university can embody all these values and more, and all parties seem to agree that it should not be confined to one. These different values reflect that there are many different stakeholders in Higher Education, which the university has to continue to respond to.

What the University does

With all these values in Higher Education it is easy to lose focus on the function the university. Its basic task is to confer degrees. To achieve that it has to recruit, guide and support students, provide effective learning environments, and to deal with all related administration, such as registration and graduation. All this requires a large workforce, and effective strategic and financial management. Hence, a modern university has to be run as a business. Like any business it is accountable both to the Government (as noted above) and to key bodies within the university itself. Universities will have different committee structures reporting to various bodies such as senate, council or court. There will be differences in function and representation from university to university. It is important for the chaplain in each institution to become aware of these structures. Many of these committees will in different ways reflect on and influence the values and identity of the particular university and they can become vital means of prophecy.

The business of a university includes managing all these stuctures, maintaining professional standards in teaching and research, and increasingly in student support. Almost by stealth the provision of student support and pastoral care has grown immensely in the last decades of the twentieth century, itself affecting the nature of the university.

The Rise of the Student Support Services

Given the way in which universities have developed it is not surprising that the question of pastoral care has changed radically. In the context of the older universities there was a strong sense of community care. Where there was a chaplain he would provide this but all academics were clergy and could provide care, a care which was strongly directive, in which values were dictated by the Church. This moved to a broader sense of *in loco parentis* in universities up to the middle of the twentieth century. Some halls of residence had 'moral tutors' whose task was to be responsible for a number of students in hall and shadow them through the year. In other universities wardens took on this moral guidance with some relish. One 'old girl' of a small hall in the University of Leeds recounts how in the late 1950s the warden would be standing at the door by 9 p.m. to make sure that all her charges were in for the night. In addition pastoral care was part of the academic remit, especially through the tutorial system.

The late twentieth century has seen the development of student-centred student support, a service increasingly offered centrally. This is partly in response to a contract and customer culture, partly in response to legislation, and partly in response to the sheer size of the modern university. Two examples illustrate this:

The University Health Service

The first student health service was set up in Edinburgh in 1930, with most universities following suit by the late 1940s, or early 50s. Until this time it was assumed that their local GPs would treat students and that there were no radically different needs. Any medical work on campus was confined to prevention and health education. The work of Edinburgh and of the American universities, especially at Yale and Michigan, helped student health services to focus on the community aspect of health and on the mental health field.

Such an approach to health meant that many doctors did not confine themselves to the surgery, serving on different university committees for instance. Often the style was patient-centred. They were concerned above all to give time to the student and thus enable her to take charge of her own health care. Such stress on student autonomy was quite the opposite of the 'medical model' of health that relied on the provision of drugs and the passive patient, with speedy 'throughput'. In addition there was greater attention to systematically assessing student need and targeting response.

Increasingly such a specialized approach to student health has been the subject of cutbacks, with universities aiming less for the community approach but rather a specialist approach through working closely with local practices, or having an advisory health team. In some cases there is a services level agreement between the local practice and the university. The importance of having such a medical provision is reinforced at times such as the outbreaks of meningitis in the 1990s.

Student Counselling

The university counselling services in many ways grew out of the national movement that led to the establishment of counselling in general in the 1960s and 70s. It was also fuelled by the rise of the new universities and polytechnics. In line with the philosophy of the time they saw themselves as much more 'student centred' than the established universities, and aimed to expand the services for students. It was hoped that the provision of such services would attract more students (Robinson 2004).

At the same time many members of the staff at new institutions had come from industry or schools where they had experienced the 'benefit to individuals of personal attention' (Robinson 2004). Counsellors in this mode were part of the wider student services and managed by them. This was very much about both staff and customer care.

The professionalization of the service nationally was set on a firm footing in 1970 with the establishment of the Association of Student Counsellors (ASC). This was later to become part of the British Association of Counselling. The ASC set about working for the development of student counselling, both through raising awareness of what they had to offer, and through the development of training and accreditation schemes.

Developments such as these were driven by an increased sense of responsibility for the mental health of the student (CVCP 2000), legislation, and concern for customer care. There was also a strong pressure from government to retain students, and to provide appropriate care for the non-traditional student coming to university through widening participation. All this led to:

- Increased professionalization and specialization of care.
- Increased centralization of care, especially in response to the larger institutions.
- Increased management of care. This was confirmed by the development in the 1980s of the Association of Managers of Student Services in Higher Education (AMOSSHE).
- A concomitant decrease in the provision of broader pastoral care, such as full-time wardens for halls of residence.

Religion in Higher Education

With all this support we might be tempted to ask where religion and chaplaincy in particular comes in. With the rise of the 'secular university' there has been a variety of different responses. Some have been suspicious. The Committee of Vice Chancellors and Principal (now Universities UK), for instance, produced a report in 1998 on extremism and intolerance on campuses, including interracial and interreligious concerns. However, as Gilliat-Ray (2000, 96) notes there are many perspectives in different universities, from anti-religious to tolerant of religions, to anti-denominational. Later universities add the perspective of multifaith pragmatist, recognizing distinctive needs of different faiths.

The provision of chaplains is a relatively recent phenomenon, emerging in Oxbridge as Higher Education was opened out. Outside Oxbridge the Church for the most part concentrated on financial support for student accommodation. In 1947 an Anglican report argued that this was not the best way to provide pastoral care for Christian students and that chaplains should be appointed. In 1954 the Church Assembly (now the General Synod) agreed to set aside money for appointing chaplains to universities. The diocese would appoint and pay stipends; the Chaplaincies Advisory Group would co-ordinate and train chaplains. By 1985 the eight university Anglican chaplains outside Oxbridge had grown to cover most of the institutes of Higher Education throughout England. In that year a full-time Secretary to Higher Education was appointed as part of the Church of England Board of Education. The concern was very much in response to the growing HE sector and in the belief, expressed by the Bishop of London in 1954 that parish clergy would find it difficult to 'get at' the student population (Thom 1987, 7).

During this time chaplaincy moved from the parish model, essentially a gathered congregation, with some outreach to the university, to much greater involvement in the structures of the university. The polytechnic chaplains contributed greatly to the development of the chaplaincy models, not least because they had to ply their ministry in inhospitable environments where there was not space or time to gather any congregation.

The polytechnic chaplains were trying to come to grips with a very different experience of Higher Education, elements of which are now firmly part of all Higher Education. Several developments have come from this:

• Faced by the sheer size of mass education chaplaincy has been increasingly focused around ecumenical cooperation. This was supported by the development of the Chaplaincy to Higher Education Liaison Group (CHELG).

- The increasingly limited resources of the churches have led to alternatives to full-time chaplains being explored, including non-stipendiary ministers, work-based priests and part-time chaplains.
- There has been increasing debate about the professional identity of chaplains and how that relates to the other support professions (Robinson and Baker 2004).
- There has been uncertainty for some local churches about the nature of the chaplaincy enterprise. This is occasionally expressed in terms of expectation conflict (Thom 1987). The Church may see chaplaincy as mission in the sense of the bringing in students, while the university may see it as a useful addition to student welfare. As Chapter 6 pointed out, this also raises questions about the nature of pastoral care.
- There has been increasing dialogue about the possibility of interfaith chaplaincy.

Further Education

With the development of Higher Education in terms of vocation, lifelong learning, skills and employability, the relationship of Higher to Further Education has become very important. Since 2001 the Learning and Skills Council has been responsible for post-sixteen education and training. This sector has over four million students, far more than Higher Education. Further Education colleges provide more Higher Education than the whole of the university sector provided in the 1960s. This will increase, not least through the development of two-year foundation degrees. FE colleges deliver almost half of the vocational qualifications in the UK. Moreover, FE provides a great number university entrants. The role of FE in stimulating and developing what Ford (1999) refers to as the 'desire for wisdom' is immense. Hence, as you would expect, the delivery of education is immensely flexible and the population is immensely diverse.

Developments in FE and the clear intention of the Government (*The Future of Higher Education* 2003, 67) to ensure close collaboration sound in one sense the final death knell of the elitist view of university education. What come first are the students, their development and needs, and the social and community context of their learning in terms of employability.

Conclusion

In many respects the history of post-compulsory education in the UK has been about widening participation, culminating in the Government setting the target of 50 per cent of the 18–30 population to be in HE by 2010.

References

Barnett, R., *The Idea of Higher Education*, Society for Research into Higher Education and Open University Press, Buckingham, 1990.

Bebbington, D., 'The Secularization of British Universities since the Mid-Nineteenth Century', in Longfield, B. and Marsden, G. (eds), *The Secularization of the Academy*, Oxford University Press, Oxford, 1992, pp. 259–77.

Bender, T., 'Pluralism and Values', in Katulushi, C. and Robinson, S. (eds), *Values in Higher Education*, University of Leeds Press, Leeds, 2004.

CVCP, *Guidelines on Student Mental Health Policies and Procedures in Higher Education*, 2000.

Escobar, M. and Freire, P., *Paulo Freire on Higher Education*, State University of New York Press, New York, 1994.

The Future of Higher Education, Cm. 5735, January 2003.

Gilliat-Ray, S., *Religion in Higher Education*, Ashgate, Aldershot, 2000.

Graham, G., *Universities: The Recovery of an Idea*, Imprint Academic, Thorverton, 2002.

Hardy, D., 'Theology in the Public Domain', a paper given at HE Chaplains' Conference, Hoddesden, 9 September, 1992.

Higher Education: The Report of the Committee appointed by the Prime Minister under the chairmanship of Lord Robbins 1961–6, HMSO, London, 1963.

Higher Education Funding Council for England (HEFCE), 'Overview of Recent Developments in HE', report no. M2/94 HEFCE, Bristol, 1994.

Jenkins, D., 'What is the Purpose of a University – and what light does Christian faith shed on this question?', *Studies in Higher Education* 13 (3), 1988, pp. 239–47.

Maskell, D. and Robinson, I., *The New Idea of a University*, Imprint Academic, Thorverton, 2002.

Megone, C. and Robinson, S., *Case Histories in Business Ethics*, Routledge, London, 2002.

National Committee of Enquiry into Higher Education, chaired by Lord Dearing, 1997.

Newman, J. H., *The Idea of a University* (ed. Svaglic), University of Notre Dame Press, Notre Dame, 1983.

Robinson, S. and Baker, N., 'The Professionalization of Higher Education Chaplaincy', for publication in *Modern Believing*, 2004.

Robinson, S., 'A very peculiar practice . . . student and staff support at the University of Leeds', in Aspden, K. (ed.), *A History of the University of Leeds*, University of Leeds Press, Leeds, 2004.

Tawney, R. H., *Equality*, Allen and Unwin, London, 1930.

Thom, K., 'Summary of B. Morgan PhD thesis: Anglican University Chaplains, University of Wales, 1986', Church of England, London, 1987.

Thomson, A., 'Elite 19 to set own pay agenda', *Times Higher Educational Supplement*, 25 July 2003, p. 1.

White, J., 'Philosophy and the Aim of Higher Education', *Studies in Higher Education*, 22(1), 1996, pp. 7–19.

Williams, R., 'Faith in the University', in Katalushi, C. and Robinson, S. (eds), *Values in Higher Education*, University of Leeds Press, Leeds, 2004.

Glossary

Alumni. Previous students of the university. Each university has an organization that keeps in contact with the alumni. It can provide an important network for chaplaincy.

Ang-Meth Soc. Anglican-Methodist Society. This was popular in some universities in the 1970s and 1980s.

Association of Student Counsellors (ASC). The ASC was developed as the national body for university and college counsellors. It became a section of the BACP (the British Association of Counsellors and Psychotherapists) and is now renamed the Association of University and College Counsellors (AUCC).

Association of University Teachers (AUT). The university teachers' professional union.

Cath Soc. Student Society for Roman Catholic Students. Like the Christian Union this is usually a society of the student union. Unlike most Christian student societies it is denominationally centred.

Centres (academic). Interdisciplinary centres for teaching and research around a common area of concern. One example is a centre of business and professional ethics, which includes input from philosophy, theology, economics, business, healthcare, medicine, law, engineering and healthcare.

Christian Medical Fellowship. An evangelical Christian group for medical students.

Cult. Cults, or New Religious Movements are organizations concerned with religion or general personal development. They are characterized by:

- a narrow and exclusive view of truth, based around a strong leader

- practice that encourages over-dependency on the group
- a negative view of families and other religious groups.

Enterprise in Higher Education. A government initiative begun in 1988 aiming at developing Higher Education, through mutually agreed processes of curriculum change, with the aim of producing more enterprising students.

ERASMUS Programme. A student mobility scheme which supports visits to European Union universities of between three and twelve months.

European directives. These refer to the Employment Equality (Religion or Belief) Regulations, 2003, Statutory instrument 1660. Section 20 of this makes it unlawful to discriminate against a student because of religion or belief, by refusing access to benefits, by excluding from the educational establishment, or by 'subjecting him to any other detriment'.

Freshers' week. See Intro-week.

Higher Education Funding Council for England. HEFCE distributes public money for teaching and research to universities and colleges. It aims to promote high quality research and education, ensuring accountability and promoting good practice.

Higher Education/Further Education. Traditionally, Higher Education deals with research and learning at degree standard. Such degrees can be vocational or not. Further Education Colleges have dealt exclusively with vocational learning and training through qualifications such as Higher National Diplomas. While that distinction broadly remains, the differences between the two sectors are becoming increasingly blurred. Firstly, Further Education is part of a broader Learning and Skills sector, including sixth-form colleges, specialist colleges and colleges of art and design. Secondly, Higher Education is exploring more and more the skills agenda, including the development of Foundation degrees (two year degrees which focus on practice and skills). Thirdly, Further Education is working more closely with Higher Education, delivering, for instance, Access courses, which might be part of a degree.

Inter textual dialogue. Dialogue between different world views or narratives that enables the development of awareness of other perspectives and the testing of one's own, as person or group. It is an important part of moral development.

Intro-week. The welcome week for new students, when they are bombarded with every possible piece of advice and advertising that can be imagined.

NGO. Non-governmental organization, such as Christian Aid, which works for justice, peace or the relief of poverty.

Personal development planning and profile. PDP is a structured and supported process undertaken by students to reflect on their own learning and achievement and to plan for their personal, educational and career development.

Services level agreement (SLA). A contract made which specifies services supplied to an organization.

SPEAK. A fairly recent evangelical group which aims to campaign and pray on issues of justice.

Student Action. A student union community action group.

Student Christian Movement (SCM). A Christian student organization of a liberal persuasion.

Student union societies. The student union provides the setting for most of the major student societies. They can be registered if they have a minimum number of students, and benefits include a degree of financial support. This provides good support for Christian student groups. However, if a new one wishes to register it will need to make very clear how it differs from any established Christian student society.

UKCOSA. The Council for International Education.

Universities and Colleges Christian Fellowship (UCCF). The national organization of the Christian Union.

Universities UK. The group which represents vice-chancellors and principals of universities in the United Kingdom, formerly CVCP (Committee of Vice-Chancellors and Principals).

Index